Let My People Go

with

Martin Luther King Jr.

Let My People Go
with
Martin Luther King Jr.

Charles Ringma

Regent College Publishing
www.regentpublishing.com

For Van Ram Oke (U Ba Oo) and Sa Lian Kai (Daw Moe Khine), prophetic servants of Christ in Myanmar (Burma)

Published 2008 by Regent College Publishing
5800 University Boulevard, Vancouver, BC V6T 2E4 Canada
Web: www.regentpublishing.com
E-mail: info@regentpublishing.com

Book design by Robert Hand
<roberthandcommunications.com>

Regent College Publishing is an imprint of the Regent Bookstore <www.regentbookstore.com>. Views expressed in works published by Regent College Publishing are those of the author and do not necessarily represent the official position of Regent College <www.regent-college.edu>.

Library and Archives Canada Cataloguing in Publication

Ringma, Charles
Let my people go with Martin Luther King Jr. / Charles Ringma.
Includes bibliographical references.
ISBN 978-1-57383-421-6
1. King, Martin Luther Jr., 1929–1968—Meditations. 2. Devotional calendars. I. Title.
BX6455.K56R56 2008 242'.2 C2008-901741-2

Contents

Preface / 9
Introduction / 11
Introducing Dr. Martin Luther King Jr. / 13

Reflections 1 to 120 / 19

Appendix: A Brief Chronology
of the Life Dr. Martin Luther King Jr. / 259
Endnotes / 267
Bibliography / 273
About the Author / 275

Preface

This book of meditations and reflections based on the writings, sermons, speeches and correspondence of Martin Luther King Jr. is part of a series that engages some of the key Christian thinkers and activists of our modern world. *Seize the Day* focuses on the writings and praxis of Dietrich Bonhoeffer. *Dare to Journey* engages the thoughts and personal explorations of Henri Nouwen. *Resist the Powers* interacts with the dialectical thinker Jacques Ellul. And *Wash the Feet of the World* reflects on the spirituality and service of Mother Teresa.

Martin Luther King Jr. is an appropriate addition to this series. Not only was he the great civil rights leader of the modern world, but he was preeminently a pastor and preacher. He was also a careful wordsmith, and much of his language is evocative, visionary and transformative.

King held a doctorate in theology, won the Nobel Peace Prize in 1964, and was not only key in the fight to overthrow racial segregation and discrimination in the United States, but also was a key campaigner against war and poverty.

Influenced by the Jesus of the Gospels and Mahatma Gandhi, King fine-tuned the practice of nonviolent resistance. He was the great proponent of peaceful means to bring about justice, peace and social transformation.

There is much in his writings, speeches, sermons and correspondence that calls for careful and reflective listening. There we find the voice of wisdom, the prophetic challenge, the call to action and the heart cry of prayer. There is the cry of pain. The vision of hope. The courage to face disappointment. And above all, the profound desire to be God's servant to a divided, bigoted, unjust and war-torn world. In listening to this voice of courage, we too can find inspiration and hope in a world where fear and violence so often strike the dominant key.

Two comments on the use of language in this book: First, in the interest of brevity, throughout the 120 reflections in this book we have dropped the "Jr." from King's name. Second, King speaks about "man" when obviously he is talking about the human person, and about "Negroes" when he is speaking about African-Americans. I have changed King's use of language to reflect contemporary usage.

This book is dedicated to my two dear friends, Van Ram Oke and his wife Sa Lian Kai, who in the Spirit of Jesus Christ and in the example of Martin Luther King Jr. seek to be God's servants of change and transformation in Myanmar.

Some thanks are in order. First of all, my deep gratitude to Mollie Rieck, my tutorial assistant at Regent College, who has helped with some of the research. She, together with Marina Ringma-McLaren, who did the computer work, are sincerely thanked for helping to bring this book to birth.

Finally, I am thankful that Regent College Publishing has made this book available in a new edition, and grateful to Robert Hand for his creativity in turning a typescript into an attractive book.

Charles Ringma
Regent College, Vancouver

Introduction

There are some who think that the vision, thoughts and speeches of Dr. Martin Luther King Jr. are passé. After all, they are quick to point out, has racial integration not occurred and has the bigotry of an earlier era not all but disappeared?

There is clearly some truth in these observations. Some things have improved. But this is not the whole story.

There is much that has not changed. The vision of King was not simply one of legislative change, but one of moral, social, economic and spiritual transformation. Moreover, he did not have only the situation of the African-Americans in view, but also the ethical renewal of his nation and the triumph of justice in the whole world.

As I pen these introductory comments in Yangon, Myanmar, where the Burmese live under an oppressive military dictatorship, the thoughts and words of Martin Luther King Jr. are as relevant as ever.

But they are also relevant in other parts of the globe where the vision for redemption in Christ, reconciliation among people groups, and the vision for shalom and justice remain as distant as ever. In many places the good news of God's desire to restore all things remains a whisper and whimper. And in many places in our world the voice of the King of Peace has been drowned out by the drumbeat of war.

Also in our Western world, the words of King are as relevant as our daily news and our daily bread. The vision for a peaceful and just society brought about by the transforming power of the gospel is as far off as ever. And in the Western world it is becoming ever distant as Western societies move away from the Man of Galilee to follow the heroes of sport, culture and science.

At this point you might well ask, "Are these the difficult things I should be thinking and praying about? Are these the things I should be reflective about? Would it not be better to focus on God and heaven so that I can survive here?"

The answer in this meditational reader to these very important questions is threefold. Yes, we do need to think about God and the ways and the purposes of his kingdom and his gospel. And yes, we do need to pray. There is so much that is beyond us. We need God's help and presence with us so much. But at the same time, we do need to wrestle with the issues of our age and time. And we do need to face the brokenness and injustice of our world.

Consequently, this meditational reader is not a book on social action. Instead, it constantly invites us to turn to God and to listen to his wisdom. It also calls us to lament, to cry, to pray. And finally, it invites us to enter the fray. It calls us to action. It invites us to practice love, mercy and justice. It calls us to prophetic resistance and transforming action. It invites us to heal and to serve.

Introducing Dr. Martin Luther King Jr.

Dr. Martin Luther King Jr. is one of the great figures of the twentieth century. His claim to fame arose from the outstanding leadership he provided for the civil rights movement in the United States in the 1950s and 1960s. This movement sought to overcome the many forms of discrimination against African-Americans and sought to gain their full political and social rights.

Through his powerful and visionary oratory and his careful strategizing, including the adaptation of nonviolent resistance as formulated by Mahatma Gandhi, King was the key bearer of the hopes and aspirations of millions of African-Americans, who experienced a second-class citizenship in a land of democratic dreams.

For this outstanding work, King was awarded the Nobel Peace Prize on December 10, 1964. He was only thirty-five years of age. Less than four years later, on April 4, 1968, King was felled by a sniper's bullet while talking on the balcony of the second floor of the Lorraine Motel in Memphis.

In these final, all-too-brief few years, King had broadened his focus to include the poverty and housing issues of African-Americans living in the northern states and resistance to his country's involvement in the Vietnam War.

So what, you may ask, does this civil rights activist have to do with a meditational reader on Christian spirituality? The brief answer is, Everything.

King came from a lineage of Baptist preachers in America's South. At eighteen he was already licensed to preach in his father's church in Atlanta. Some seven years later, King was installed as pastor of Dexter Avenue Church in Montgomery. The following year he completed his PhD in systematic theology from Boston University. It was in Montgomery that King was elected as president of the Montgomery Improvement Association, which organized the bus boycott over segregated buses. This drew King into the fray of the civil rights movement.

Therefore King was both a preacher and a political activist. He was a Christian who held a theological vision that allowed him to be God's servant in both spheres of life—the ecclesiastical and the societal.

Committed to the biblical vision of love and justice, King was able to work and strategize to bring about social change, while at the same time resisting the path of hatred and vengeance toward one's enemies.

So why then should one engage King in this meditational reader? Have things not radically changed in the United States, and do African-Americans not experience full equality? And if I am not all that concerned about social issues, will King have anything to say to me? Can I take King on a spiritual retreat and learn something from him?

Let me make some responses to these questions.

Yes, a lot has changed since the 1950s and 1960s in terms of political rights and freedoms. But there is much in our world that has not changed. Racism, discrimination, poverty, militarism and injustice are still a part of our world.

In the face of the persistence of evil, it is easy to become fatalistic and to conclude, This is the way things are! One can also become passive: There is little use in trying to change anything! And it is equally tempting for Christians to become inward-looking and to embrace a world-denying, rather than a world-formative, type of Christianity.

King's writings and speeches point us in a very different direction. He points to a vision of the kingdom of God that brings God's shalom to every sphere of life, including the racial and the economic. And in line with the Old Testament prophetic tradition and the ministry of Jesus, King calls us to engagement. We are not called to accept the way things are, but to pray and work so that God's kingdom of love and justice may more fully come among us.

Because racism, poverty and injustice are still evident in our world, King's vision for social transformation remains an enduring one. And because his social activism came out of a theological vision, King's abiding contribution will be to remind us that following Christ has social and political implications. The love of Christ is a love that calls us into the public sphere.

King was a pastor and a preacher. Throughout his life he saw himself in these terms. And throughout his writings and speeches there sparkles the biblical vision of God's redemption, a spirituality of hope, the power of love and forgiveness, the courage to act, and the need to pray. One can gain much from the pastoral wisdom of this servant of the gospel.

In using this book as a meditational reader for daily prayer and reflection or for a time of retreat, there are some outstanding themes that one will encounter.

King's life demonstrates that God's purposes for our life are often far greater than we anticipate. Thus we are called to surrender ourselves to the way of God with our life in joyful obedience.

King's life and message show us that while the way of love—including love for one's enemies—appears to be the way of weakness, it is the way that overcomes. This is the way of Christ. It is the way of the Cross. It is also the way we are called to live.

One of King's abiding themes is that suffering for the cause of Christ's way of reconciliation and peace is never in vain. Suffering is redemptive. Fruit will come from those who give their lives in the service of Christ for the sake of their neighbor.

Finally, King's vision of life, while pragmatic, was fundamentally eschatological. His vision was not what is, but what can be. And this vision was as broad as the biblical hope for the renewal and restoration of all things. King saw a world where all could sit at the banquet table. Welcome for all. Dignity for all. Provision for all.

Let's hear King's words. In his famous "I Have a Dream" speech of 1963, he exclaimed, "I have a dream that one day on the red hills of Georgia sons [and daughters] of former slaves and sons [and daughters] of former slave-owners will be able to sit down together at the table of brotherhood [and sisterhood]." And in his last sermon in 1968, entitled "I See the Promised Land," King stated, "I would like to live a long life. . . . But I'm not concerned about that now. I just want to do God's will."

This meditational reader invites you into the heart, passion and praxis of Dr. Martin Luther King Jr. It also invites you into the biblical story and the theological vision that undergirded King's prophetic life and mission.

As such, this reflective reader invites you into a socially relevant spirituality, into the power to resist the world's agenda, into the courage to live and act prophetically, and into the passion to dream God's hope for our world and for the world to come.

I

The Seeking God

Knowing the God Who Seeks and Finds Us

The God of the Bible is not a remote autocrat who inhabits the heavens. God is the God of the Exodus, the prophets, the Incarnation. God is the God who enters history and takes the pain and folly of history upon himself to transform it into his shalom.

Fundamental to the human quest has been the search for transcendence, hope and transformation. In an earlier world, that quest was primarily expressed in religious terms. In our modern world, the quest has taken on many forms in the shape of political ideologies, technology and scientism, and the hope of material progress.

In culture's most recent detour, the human quest has once again reverted to the exploration of more spiritual values. But, sadly, in the general community there is great ambivalence toward the God of the Bible and the project called Christianity. Because Christianity is seen as beholden to modernity and its values of rationality, power and control, the God of the Bible is seen as oppressive at worst, and irrelevant at best.

That the God of the Bible is *very different* is a vision that needs to be rediscovered.

While we may wish that this rediscovery could somehow occur apart from the church and the church's witness to the world (and there are times when this has occurred), this is far too cheap a hope. The God of the Bible has to be rediscovered deep within the community of faith. And from that new center, light shines in church and world. In other words, the church is responsible for how the world understands who God is.

Martin Luther King was convinced that the God of the Bible seeks us out. And that God penetrates the hardest and most difficult places. He writes that God "seeks us in dark places and suffers with us and for us in our tragic prodigality."[1] These dark places are not only the places of sin and fear. They are also the places of conformity. They are the places where we are beholden to the seemingly innocent idols of our time. They are also the places of indifference.

The God of the Bible joins us to forgive and heal. But also to transform. And this transformation can only align us with God's purposes to renew humanity by his love and grace. When we rediscover the depth of the love of God, our witness to an indifferent world will be all the more telling.

Reflection: "My ears had heard of you but now my eyes have seen you. Therefore I despise myself and repent in dust and ashes" (Job 42:5–6).

2

Servant of Greatness

The Social Ethics of the Kingdom of God

Leadership, power and mastery are significant dimensions of our social world. But so easily these dynamics can be used for self-aggrandizement rather than for the greater good of others. As such, these important elements need to be converted to the ethics of the reign of God.

The world has seen all sorts of leaders. A Nero and a Constantine. A Hitler and a Gandhi. A Pinochet and a Mother Teresa. Leadership is one of God's good general gifts to humanity, a gift of God's common grace. Through the good use of this gift, people are given a vision, they are mobilized, and new social realities come into being. Through its misuse, oppression occurs and people suffer under its harshness and cruelty.

The Bible is full of people with amazing leadership skills. A Moses. A Deborah. A David. A Nehemiah. These leaders led Israel to liberation, victory and renewal. But the Bible also knows of another form of leadership. That of Jeremiah and many of the other prophets, and that of Jesus. These were the suffering-servant leaders who took to heart the difficult call of God to be a voice of repentance and renewal to a wayward people. Clearly, Martin Luther King belongs to a contemporary version of this type of leadership.

King himself comments, "Everybody can be great. Because

anybody can serve."[2] Here leadership is seen in a particular way. It is a leadership committed to bringing about change through identification and service. In this Jesus is the great example. He is the Suffering Servant and the Servant King. His leadership takes to heart the failure of others and transforms that failure into a vision of forgiveness, reconciliation and peace.

True leadership brings about the new based on God's transforming shalom. It's a leadership that celebrates the reign of God and as such is a leadership that serves through suffering.

Reflection: "But he was pierced for our transgressions, he was crushed for our iniquities; the punishment that brought us peace was upon him, and by his wounds we are healed" (Isaiah 53:5).

3

All of Life

The Transformation of Individuals and Institutions

The biblical story reveals a God who offers redemption to all, but who particularly has the poor and oppressed in view. God calls the rich and powerful to his salvation and turns their hearts and hands to serve the poor.

There have been long periods in the history of the Christian church when the spiritual was elevated above the material and the soul was magnified over the body. The impression was thus given that Christianity was only concerned with the inner person and that the outward circumstances of life did not matter so much. Thus, if you were a slave, never mind, as long as you had faith in Jesus.

Martin Luther King roundly condemns this approach to life. He notes, "Religion that professes to be concerned about the souls of men [and women] and is not concerned about the economic conditions that damn the soul . . . is a dry, dead, do-nothing religion."[3]

The power of the biblical story is not that God has made a place for us in heaven, as blessed as that may be. Its power lies elsewhere. It is embedded in the fact that God does not remain idle in the face of oppression and injustice. God enters history to bring salvation and liberation.

The whole of Israel's faith is based not only on God as the Creator, but more fundamentally on the God of the Exodus.

This is the God who sets slaves free. The New Testament follows a similar theme. The good news of Jesus is good news for all. But this news is particularly embraced by those in need. The healthy, so the gospel tells us, have no need of a doctor. And the redemption Jesus brings is not simply for the soul but for the whole person and for all of life's relationships.

The powerful who come to faith can no longer oppress. And the poor who come to faith may no longer despise themselves. For in Christ and in his body, the church, they are all one. One in Christ. One in love. And one in the call to serve each other. Moreover, they are one in their challenge to the world. The old order of hierarchy and oppression has been done away with in Christ.

> *Reflection: "Perhaps the reason he was separated from you for a little while was that you might have him back for good—no longer as a slave, but better than a slave, as a dear brother" (Philemon 15–16).*

4

Open Church

The Church with Its Face Toward the World

The church can so easily breathe the rarefied air of its own exclusivity. If this is so, it is no longer the church that Jesus came to bring into being. The true church has its heart, doors and arms flung open toward the world.

The church in today's world is struggling. In our Western multicultural world, it is no longer the sole provider of religious services. The church is now simply one among many religious options. People today pick and choose. And for many, Christianity is not that attractive.

This poses a major challenge for the present-day church. And in reaction it is so easy for the church to become defensive and inward-looking.

But such a defensive posture is not good, neither for the church nor for the world. A healthy church is not a defensive institution, but a faith-risking community. And the world will never be challenged by a church that is merely self-preoccupied.

Martin Luther King once made the observation that "when the church is true to its nature, it says, 'Whosoever will, let him [or her] come.'"[4] Such a church is an open church, a witnessing church, and a serving community of faith.

To be a church with its doors and arms flung open to the world does not mean that the world sets the agenda for the church. This cannot be, for the church is called to live under the lordship of Christ and as such cannot serve two masters. But what it does mean is that the church is to hear and enter into the world's pain and need. It means that the church is willing to serve the world even when the church's message is scoffed at or rejected.

Moreover, the church's openness to the world is an unqualified openness. It is an openness to all. Rich and poor. The majority of a population and its minorities. The able and those with disabilities. This kind of openness can only flow from a deep clinging to the God of the Bible and to the vision of the gospel. Moreover, this kind of openness can only be sustained by the power of the Spirit.

Reflection: "There is neither Jew nor Greek, slave nor free, male nor female, for you are all one in Christ Jesus" (Galatians 3:28).

5

Costly Love

Living a Love That Hurts

Christ carried a love for humanity that was willing to embrace humanity's shame, folly and sin. Love made Christ the great sin-bearer. We who name Christ as our Savior and Lord are called to walk a similar path, living a love that hurts.

We live in a world of friends and foes, of family and strangers, of grace and hatred. While often these lines are clearly drawn, this is not always our experience. Sometimes the friend can become the foe. And sometimes the stranger can be the bearer of grace.

Even though life is complex and ambiguous, we nevertheless are always quick to categorize. And we are too familiar with those who are insiders and too distrusting of those who are outsiders. With our categorizations come different ways of treating people. Our own we treat with love and respect. The outsider we ignore or neglect.

The disturbing gospel of Jesus calls us to a whole different way of seeing people and of responding to them. This upside-down gospel of the reign of God challenges us to treat outsiders, even enemies, as if they were insiders.

Martin Luther King faced this challenge. His family home was bombed, and in later reflecting on this, he commented, "It is pretty difficult to like someone bombing your home. . . . But

Jesus says love them."[5] Here King recognizes the radical nature of Christian love. It is a love not simply for friends, but also for enemies. It is a love that burns not only in the fire of familiar intimacy, but burns equally bright in the hot coals of enmity and rejection.

This is no mere human love. This is God's love made recklessly abundant in the human heart. This love is fanned by the flapping wings of the Holy Spirit. That we know little of such a love is a sad comment on the spiritual emptiness of our present world and the contemporary church. Only a deeper conformity to Christ, who forgave those who crucified him, can spawn such a love into such cold hearts as ours.

Reflection: "But love your enemies, do good to them, and lend to them without expecting to get anything back. Then your reward will be great, and you will be sons of the Most High, because he is kind to the ungrateful and the wicked" (Luke 6:35).

6

Being Co-Opted

Failing to Discern and to Resist

There are two equally important dimensions to the Christian faith. One is that religion acts as a stabilizing influence in our world. The other is that it sounds a prophetic trumpet and, as such, acts as the great change agent.

The Christian faith, when it expresses the gospel that Jesus embodied and proclaimed, has much to give to our world. It can give churches an oasis of spirituality. It can produce women and men who live their lives with gentleness and generosity. It has given to the world people such as St. Augustine, Martin Luther, John Wesley, J. S. Bach, C. S. Lewis and Mother Teresa. And in giving these gifts to the world, the people of God have enhanced the world's beauty and beneficence.

But the Christian community does not only exist to give to the world religious cantatas and art. It is not simply there to enhance a general goodness and to provide stability and continuity in our social order. There is another role that the people of God are called to fulfill. They are called to be the discerners of our times, watchers on the walls of our culture.

While the church is called to affirm all that is good in our society and is to celebrate that as a sign of God's common grace, the church is also called to resist every form of evil, including the idolatries of our age. However, all too often the community of faith is too inward-looking and far too naive about what is happening in our world. As a result, it gets co-opted by the world's agenda.

While referring to a different context, namely, the earlier African-American acceptance of its own marginalization, Martin Luther King makes an important general point: "Passively to accept an unjust system is to co-operate with that system and thereby to become a participant in its evil."[6] The contemporary church is not without its failures in this regard. We need only think of the way in which the Lutheran Church in Germany was co-opted by Nazism.

So the challenge for the community of faith is to be discerning, to be courageous, and to resist the powers and idolatries of our time. And materialism and militarism are but two such evils.

We need to learn to say yes to God. But no to the worldliness of our world.

> *Reflection: "Wash and make yourselves clean. Take your evil deeds out of my sight! Stop doing wrong, learn to do right! Seek justice, encourage the oppressed. Defend the cause of the fatherless, plead the case of the widow" (Isaiah 1:16–17).*

7

The Triumph of the Good

The Long Road of Its Appearance

There are many promises in the biblical story that good will triumph over evil. But this triumph does not always come quickly or easily. And the final revelation of good will not occur in human history but in God's eschatological future.

We live in the beautiful but fragile world of nature. And the human community in all of its cultural and ethnic diversity partakes of so much that is good, but also of that which is evil and oppressive. In the midst of all of this, we often cry out, "Why does the good not prevail? Why the persistence of evil? Why is what we hope and long for so slow in coming?" These are difficult questions to answer. But one thing is clear: evil does not finally triumph. The very heyday of the triumph of evil's power is the beginning of its undoing.

In pondering the long history of African-American oppression, Martin Luther King finally came to a conclusion expressed in his Nobel Peace Prize acceptance speech: "Right temporarily defeated is stronger than evil triumphant."[7] We too may share his certainty.

This certainty does not lie only in the observation of human history, where again and again evil empires have finally collapsed and wrongdoing has been exposed. Nor do we have this certainty because there have always been men and women on the stage of history who have cried out, "Enough! This is wrong! This is intolerable! This has to stop!"

The main reason why the weakness of good is stronger than the strength of evil is that God is only supporter of the good. And while good spawns wellbeing and wholeness, evil spawns its own destruction. The clearest sign of this apparent contradiction is the cross of Christ. By all appearance Golgotha was the triumph of evil. The One who healed did not rescue himself, but embraced an awful and shameful death. Good seemed to be utterly defeated.

But sin and death were defeated in the death and resurrection of Christ. The goodness of God was triumphant, because God is the champion of all that brings life, forgiveness and wholeness.

Reflection: "Commit your way to the LORD; trust in him and he will do this: He will make your righteousness shine like the dawn, the justice of your cause like the noonday sun" (Psalm 37:5–6).

8

One in Christ

The Miracle of Reconciliation

The miracle of the power of the gospel under the inspiration of the Holy Spirit is that women and men find peace with God—but also that they find peace with each other. Thus persons and groups of people who previously were alienated from each other become reconciled. Enemies become friends.

The effect of the power and grace of Christ in our lives is that we begin to develop new attitudes toward others because something has changed within us.

We so easily typify other people who are different from us. We adorn them with negative images. We stereotype them so that we can keep them at arm's length. And if we are really honest with ourselves, we have to acknowledge that we often carry bitterness, or disdain, or even fear toward such people.

The solution to all of this, we reiterate to ourselves, is that *they* should change. *They* should become like us. But this is hardly an answer. Instead, it simply creates a stalemate. And nothing changes.

But things can begin to change when something happens in *us*. Christ can change our attitudes toward others because he can give us the gift of love, erode our fears and remove our bitterness. When this amazing work of grace takes place in *both* parties, the miracle of reconciliation bursts into view. Suspicions are broken down. Fear is displaced by love. Enemies embrace each other.

Martin Luther King reminds us that "in Christ there is neither Jew nor Gentile . . . communist nor capitalist."[8] When each of the members of these different ethnic and political groupings comes to faith in Christ, something changes. The Jew can no longer be exclusive and self-righteous, and the communist can no longer be committed to a repressive state ideology. Christ takes the blinders from our eyes and the power of ideologies from our hearts and minds. We begin to see differently and believe differently, and we begin to live differently.

The way of Christ, the way of love, the way of peace becomes the dominant reality for us and others, and so we become one by the grace and power of Christ.

Reflection: "He came and preached peace to you who were far away and peace to those who were near. For through him we both have access to the Father by one Spirit" (Ephesians 2:17–18).

9

Forgiveness

The Power of Reconciliation

In a fallen and broken world, forgiveness is as basic as bread. Because we fail others and others fail us, forgiveness becomes a necessity if the human community is to live together in hope, peace and love.

There are some who hold and promote the idea that, while forgiveness should be extended to family and friends who have hurt us in some way, forgiveness should not be extended to our oppressors and those who exploit and marginalize us. The concern that lies at the heart of this qualification is that such forgiveness gives more power to the oppressor. Therefore hatred of the oppressor is more appropriate. Hatred involves resistance, while forgiveness involves compliance.

The issue that is being addressed here is very important. The concern is not to weaken the position of the one who is already weak, nor to hurt the one who is already hurting. While this concern needs careful attention, the fundamental idea that hatred is a more powerful form of resistance is faulty. Hatred of the oppressor is finally to become like the one who dominates. Thus hatred leads to an ugly conformity to the very one from whom we seek to be free.

Moreover, it is simply not true that forgiveness involves compliance. Forgiveness never means that one accepts or justifies the wrong. In fact, forgiveness recognizes the opposite: the wrong done is so wrong that it cannot be ignored nor can it be repaid. It can only in love and grace be forgiven.

There is great power in forgiveness. To forgive another is to free oneself. It is to refuse hatred and bitterness. It is a refusal of angry retaliation that leads to coming under the sway of the perpetrator. Therefore Martin Luther King is right in saying that the one "who is devoid of the power to forgive is devoid of the power to love."[9] And to love one's enemies is not to agree with their wrongdoing but to subvert them so that they might find grace and repentance.

Reflection: "Do not repay anyone evil . . . .
Do not be overcome by evil, but overcome
evil with good" (Romans 12:17, 21).

10

Interconnectedness

Living the Miracle of Solidarity

In the Western world the rights, needs and wants of the individual have become of paramount value. While we want to celebrate the importance of each person, we also need to recognize the importance of community and to practice the challenging art of solidarity.

Martin Luther King made the observation that "we are all caught in an inescapable network of mutuality."[10] This general statement is true at every level of our social existence. We come into the world and grow up needing our parents, teachers, friends and a range of caregivers.

Everything we possess and consume has usually come to us due to the work of others. And whether it is a team sport, an interest group, or the workplace, these all function on the basis of participation and cooperation.

The Christian church also knows something about the power of interconnectedness. And it articulates this at two levels: the vertical and the horizontal.

The primary relationship is the vertical. Through the work of Christ and by the Spirit we are invited to partake of and participate in the life of the Trinity. This is the interconnectedness of transcendence. Here we seek the face of God as we practice prayer, solitude, worship and obedience.

From the vertical comes the horizontal. Through Christ, we

become members of the body of Christ. And the Spirit makes us one. This is the interconnectedness of Christian community. Here we seek to live and to serve one another. Christian community operates on the basis that we need the Spirit to infuse and to empower us and we need the giftedness of each one so we will grow into maturity and Christlikeness.

But there is another dimension to interconnectedness. We so often think we should only be linked to the powerful and strong. But this is only half the story. We also need the vulnerable ones in our midst. The poor, the marginal, those with disabilities can teach us much about humility, hope, care and perseverance.

Reflection: "The body is a unit, though it is made up of many parts; and though all its parts are many, they form one body. So it is with Christ. For we were all baptized by one Spirit into one body—whether Jews or Greeks, slave or free—and we were all given the one Spirit to drink" (1 Corinthians 12:12–13).

11

A Voice Crying

The Pain of the Prophet

There is much in our world that calls for gratitude and celebration. But there is also much that causes grief. The latter cannot be ignored. Evil in our world must not only be identified; it must also be spoken against. But more importantly, it must be resisted and overcome.

There are powerful instincts that impact all of us. One such instinct is the impulse toward self-preservation. Another is the need to be accepted and loved. When both of these powerful sentiments are taken together, it is hardly a surprise that we are oriented toward social conformity. And this so often means that we accept the status quo and resist sticking our necks out.

The prophet, on the other hand, moves in the opposite direction. He or she challenges the dominant ideologies and cries for repentance, resistance and transformation. This is no easy calling. In his resistance to the Vietnam War, Martin Luther King admitted that "the calling to speak is often a vocation of agony."[11]

There is no glory for the prophet, only the call to utter abandonment to the difficult will of God. This has significant implications. Prophets in the biblical sense of that word are not self-styled proponents of their own radical ideas. The world has had its fair share of loudmouths and egomaniacs. These don't deserve the title of prophet.

True prophets are very different. They are the reluctant spokespersons of God. They are pulled by the Spirit into the fray. They have faced their own fears and insecurities. They have counted the cost. And yet they speak. They can do no other. And the reason they can do no other is because the things about which they speak are things that belong to the dominion of darkness. They are things that need to be exposed by the search-light of God's love, mercy and justice. They are the things that destroy and that cry out for redress.

And so the prophet embraces the often-lonely task of saying what needs to be said and calling for change even when so many refuse to hear.

Reflection: "But the LORD said to me, 'Do not say, "I am only a child." You must go to everyone I send you to and say whatever I command you. Do not be afraid of them, for I am with you and will rescue you'" (Jeremiah 1:7–8).

12

Life's Heartbeat

Living the Biblical Vision

There is nothing narrow about the biblical vision of life's meaning and purpose. And we contemporary Christians must make sure that we don't diminish the scope of life lived under God's lordship, in love and service to others and in stewardship and care for all that God has created.

A world of difference lies between living a life of simplicity and simplifying things so they become manageable. The gospel calls us to embrace the former but to reject the latter. When we simplify things we are reductionistic. We flatten or remove the rich contours of a vision and of a way of life.

The contemporary church faces this challenge. It has reduced the gospel of the kingdom of God to a message that focuses only on personal salvation. It has reduced the rich vision of Christian community to consumer Christianity. And some contemporary churches have reduced the vision for the transcendent to a concern for the social dimensions of life only. Rather than simplifying, we need to recover the profound vision of life embedded in the biblical story and to live that with a simplicity of faith, hope and love.

Martin Luther King once made the observation that "the length of life . . . is . . . to achieve its personal ends and ambitions . . . the breadth of life is the outward concern for the welfare of others. The height of life is the upward reach for God."[12] There is something wonderfully whole about the biblical vision of life. It gives shape to the created order and dignity to humanity. It frames a vision of life within the themes of creation, redemption and the final consummation of all things. It sees God as the initiator and sustainer of all things and sees us as the recipients of his goodness, beneficence and grace.

This vision calls us to worship and rejoice in who God is and in all that he made. This vision calls us to enter into the healing and renewal that God offers a wounded and wayward humanity. And it calls us to form communities of faith, love and service that welcome the needy and work for restoration and peace.

Reflection: "He has showed you, O man, what is good. And what does the LORD require of you? To act justly and to love mercy and to walk humbly with your God" (Micah 6:8).

13

Arrogance

The Blinding Power of the Powerful

To be powerful brings with it an awesome responsibility and a great temptation. Power is seductive and it is only benign when it is used for good ends and for others. But when power is used for self-aggrandizement and to exploit others, it blinds and eventually destroys.

History is replete with examples of those who have misused their great power. In the ancient world we note Alexander the Great. In the modern world we are reminded of Stalin and Hitler. The more blatant the misuse of power, the easier it is to identify. But power has also been misused in subtle and ambiguous ways.

During the long project of Christendom, the church often misused its power through its opposition to new knowledge in the arts or sciences. The fate of Galileo is but one example. This opposition occurred in the name of good, namely, to safeguard the holy doctrines of the church.

Western colonialism also took place under the rubric of good, namely, to bring Christianity and a supposed superior culture to the rest of the world.

But this too was a misuse of power. The final motivation was not to bless other people but to exploit them.

In many ways, both economically and culturally, but also militarily, the long march of Western dominance continues.

And while it may claim that it exercises its power to help others, the West is, in the final analysis, sowing the seeds of its own demise. This is terribly troubling and calls for deep repentance, particularly on the part of the church in the West. But what is even more troubling is that the West has become blind to its own motivations. It is arrogant and has been blinded by its own power.

Martin Luther King spoke of Western arrogance in his day. He was critical of Western intervention in other countries and noted that the West assumed "that it has everything to teach others and [has] nothing to learn from them."[13] It is past time that Western Christians repent of their nationalism and of their countries' exploitation of the rest of the world. And that they raise their voices for a new world that is no longer scarred by war but by the Cross.

Reflection: "He will teach us his ways, so that we may walk in his paths. . . . They will beat their swords into ploughshares. . . . Nation will not take up sword against nation, nor will they train for war anymore" (Isaiah 2:3–4).

14

The Will of God

Embracing the Cost of Discipleship

Influenced by the dominant values of our culture, we sometimes foolishly think and live as if everything revolves around us, including the blessings of God. But we are not the center. God is. And the heartbeat of the Christian life is to worship and obey the God who has redeemed us. The surprise for those who walk this spiritual pilgrimage is that obedience leads to true freedom.

Martin Luther King could not have expressed the purpose of life as a Christian more clearly: "The end of life is not to be happy nor to achieve pleasure and avoid pain, but to do the will of God."[14] This goes to the very heart of the Christian story. Not only was obedience to the revealed will of Yahweh central to the Old Testament, but the very heartbeat of Jesus had to do with the joy he experienced in knowing and doing the will of his Father in heaven.

For contemporary Christians the idea of obedience is problematical. It has an oppressive ring to it in a society that celebrates consensus. You don't obey people; you come to agreement! The gospel, therefore, challenges us and calls for a recovery of a theology of obedience.

At the heart of the biblical story, the call to obey God does not spring from God's coercive nature but from the generosity of his grace toward us. The God we are called to obey is the God who loves us in Jesus Christ and who gave his life for our salvation, healing and recovery. Furthermore, the God we are called to obey is the God of all knowledge and wisdom, who in his sovereign love and power does know what is best for us. Therefore, to obey God is both a grateful response to God's grace and an act of wisdom.

Obedience always has two dimensions. We are called to obey God's revelation in Scripture, and we are called to obey the leading of the Holy Spirit. The former is the general will of God. The latter is the more specific and personal. These are not to be played off against each other. We obey the one will of God made specific in the circumstances in which we live.

This is to be the heartbeat of our life. It is an acknowledgement of Christ the King.

Reflection: "But if anyone obeys his word, God's love is truly made complete in him. This is how we know we are in him: Whoever claims to live in him must walk as Jesus did" (1 John 2:5–6).

15

A Whole Gospel

Good News for the Whole Person

While in the West we operate with either/or categories and the church in the West has been affected by dualistic thinking, this is not so in the biblical story. The spiritual and the material are not played off against each other. God is both creator and redeemer. God's blessing is for the whole person and the whole community. We urgently need to recover this vision of the sacredness of all life.

There are powerful signals throughout the whole of the biblical story that no dimension of life is unimportant to God and that all of life is to be impregnated with the presence of the Holy Spirit. Moreover, the salvation God offers us by his grace is to save the whole of who we are, to renew all of what we are, and to make whole every dimension of our lives and our relationships.

Martin Luther King sums this up well: "The gospel at its best deals with the whole person, not only his or her soul but body [as well], not only his or her spiritual well-being but the material [as well]."[15] This perspective has significant implications for Christian preaching and teaching as well as for the mission and ministry of the church in the world. The teaching of the church, therefore, cannot be ecclesio-centric. Its focus is to be the outworking of the reign of God in all of life. Preaching has to do with the good news of God's healing in Christ of the whole creation. All of life is being made new in Christ.

And the mission of the church is the whole people of God bringing the whole gospel to the world. The church is the missional people of God. All are servants of the King and all are called to be witnesses of the reign of God and the gospel of the kingdom.

Serving Christ the King in all of life becomes our sacred calling. Christians in the pulpit and Christians in politics. Christians in the monastery and Christians in the stock exchange. Christians at prayer and Christians at play. Christians in the home and Christians at work. All seeking to honor God, seeking to serve their neighbors and colleagues, and seeking to be salt and leaven and light in all human activity. We're called to all of this, so that God's shalom may penetrate our hearts and our communities.

Reflection: "You are the light of the world. A city on a hill cannot be hidden. Neither do people light a lamp and put it under a bowl. Instead they put it on its stand, and it gives light to everyone in the house. In the same way, let your light shine before men, that they may see your good deeds and praise your Father in heaven" (Matthew 5:14–16).

16

With God

Empowerment from the God Who Journeys with Us

An active sense of the presence of God is not a grace that we always experience. In our modern world so dependent on human technology and achievement, God often seems remote. And even in our churches our sense of Immanuel, God with us, is often weak. Thus we are challenged to a deeper spirituality where we live the truth that God is with us and in us.

Many people in our contemporary world hold the opinion that God does not exist. The idea of God, they claim, is a mythological leftover of earlier and now outmoded worldviews. Others are not quite so sure. They hold some belief in God, but this makes no practical difference to their lives and values. But for others, the idea of God is not only important, the existence of God is not only relevant, but the presence of God in their lives is essential to who they are and to everything they do.

Martin Luther King puts this quite starkly: "Without God all of our efforts turn to ashes and our sunrises into darkest nights. . . . With God we are able to rise from the midnight of desperation to the daybreak of joy."[16] This expresses not some general sense that it is good to have God around, like a policeman in a crowd, but that God is essential to our lives, to our hopes and dreams. At its heart, this perspective holds that we can't live without God's help, grace and power.

This vision lies at the heart of the biblical story. The Old Testament people were to trust Yahweh as their provider. Jesus was fully dependent on his Father in heaven. The apostle John spoke of God living in us and we in him. And the apostle Paul stressed the importance of being in Christ through the power of the Spirit. Simply put, we are called to live in God and for God. God sustains our life, and we orient our life toward him in faith and obedience.

God with us and in us does not make us superhuman. This is not a position of triumphalism. Rather, it is a position of faith and trust that we want to live in and for God in all that we do.

God with us does not put us in a place of privilege but in the position of serving the purposes of God in our time and in our world.

Reflection: "I am the vine; you are the branches. If a man remains in me and I in him, he will bear much fruit; apart from me you can do nothing" (John 15:5).

17

The Contrary Voice

Resisting and Challenging the Powers of This Age

While Christians are to build families and to contribute to the social, economic and cultural good of the society of which they are a part—and while they are also to witness, build up the community of faith, and create institutions that serve the wider society—they are a people, nevertheless, who are out of step with the dominant values of their culture. They have been captured by a different vision and march to the beat of a different drummer.

Far too often the church through its long two-thousand-year journey has blended in to its social and cultural landscape and has been the supporter of the political status quo. The result has been a cultural Christianity characterized by blandness and conformity.

There were also periods in the history of the Christian church when the light of the kingdom of God shone brightly and the church was a powerful prophetic voice in the society of that time. We need only think of the Reformation and the Wesleyan revival as two of many examples.

Yet the church's role in the wider society will always be an ambivalent one: it is called to affirm the good but to resist and overcome evil. King is helpful in identifying the basic stance of the church. He notes, "The church must be reminded that it is not the master or servant of the state, but rather the conscience of the state."[17] In order for the community of faith to play such a role in society, some things need to be in place.

The first is that Christians must have a perspective on life that involves economic, cultural and political issues. Some Christians think they should be concerned only with spiritual matters. Yet God's lordship involves all of life, not simply his lordship over the soul.

Second, the church must be shaped by a vision of God's peaceable kingdom and by his righteousness, mercy and justice. It is only as the church inhabits the gospel that it will have a vision that is different from the dominant values in the culture.

And finally, if the church is to speak courageously and prophetically to society, it must first of all *live* prophetically. The church, therefore, needs to embody its prophecy and in its life together anticipate what it desires the society to become.

Reflection: "Of the increase of his government and peace there will be no end. He will reign on David's throne and over his kingdom, establishing and upholding it with justice and righteousness from that time on and forever. The zeal of the L*ORD* *Almighty will accomplish this" (Isaiah 9:7).*

18

The Cross

Symbol of Shame, Symbol of Hope

The Cross stands at the very center of the Christian story. In and of itself, the Cross is the symbol of shame. In the gospel, the Cross is the reality of a great injustice, but it is also the symbol of hope. The shameful death of Christ, the innocent One, becomes the way of salvation for all who put their faith and trust in him.

In a world so full of the reality of death, including death through war and poverty, it is ironic that we do everything we can to avoid the subject. Particularly in Western culture, death is the great reality we refuse to face. But death is not only intrinsic to life itself; it is also at the heart of the biblical story. The Cross is central to the gospel. Martin Luther King believed that "the cross is the eternal expression of the length to which God will go in order to restore broken community."[18]

This is a good insight. It has to do with the amazing self-giving of God. God gives himself in the incarnation in his Son. God gives himself in Christ to a cruel death to bring reconciliation to the world. This reflects the great Pauline truth that God was in Christ "reconciling the world to himself" (2 Corinthians 5:19). The death of the One, Jesus Christ—the Innocent One—brings life for all, the guilty ones.

The Cross is also at the center of the church. By this I do not mean on its buildings' spires, but in the Eucharist or Lord's

Supper. In that sacramental feast the church participates in and remembers the death of Christ and the blessings that flow from Christ's self-giving.

But the life of the church and that of its members is also to be marked by the Cross. The Christian life is cruciform. What does this mean? The cross of Christ not only brings forgiveness and new life to us; it also brings with it a death to our old ways of being and doing. And the Cross also works in us a willingness to sacrifice and to relinquish much more the sake of the gospel.

Thus we too have to bear the cross. In our commitment to the will of the Father in heaven and to his purposes for our world, we too will have to walk the road of service and suffering. For some, this may mean the gift of martyrdom, but for all it is the gift of sacrificial service.

Reflection: "For Christ's love compels us, because we are convinced that one died for all, and therefore all died. And he died for all, that those who live should no longer live for themselves but for him who died for them and was raised again" (2 Corinthians 5:14–15).

19

Resisting the Easy Way

Replacing Hatred with Forgiveness

At the very heart of the moral universe lies the wonder of forgiveness. Because we are all less than perfect and fail others, forgiveness is something we need to receive from others and extend to others. The God of the Bible is the God who forgives, heals and reconciles. We are invited to extend that same grace to others.

Hatred is a powerful human emotion that can have far-reaching consequences for ourselves as well as others. It can lead to the rejection of the other person. It can also lead to harming that person. Often hatred leads to various forms of aggression and violence.

While hatred may come from a place of sheer irrationality when no one has harmed us, it usually comes from a place of retaliation. We have been wrongly hurt in some way and so lash out to hurt those who have wronged us.

Hatred is often not the sole province of the individual. It has a way of spreading. It is infectious. It pulls others into its orbit and spell. The person who hates often draws allies into his or her circle of hatred.

Thus hatred is often communal. Not only are individuals harmed or hurt by others, but families, communities, people groups and even nations can experience harm and rejection.

Breaking the cycle of hatred is breaking one of the most destructive forces in our lives, communities and world. Because hatred infects and affects both the hater and the one hated, all are losers; all become ensnared.

The witness of Martin Luther King on this matter is exemplary. He wrote, "I've seen too much hate to want to hate, [and] hate is too great a burden to bear."[19] Having been himself the victim of racial hatred, King was committed to breaking the cycle. For him the source and motivation for doing this was the call of Jesus to forgive, even one's enemies. But there was also the recognition that hatred adds to the burden and dehumanization of the one who hates.

There is no victory in hatred. All lose. Only in the gentle practice of forgiveness lie freedom and hope, not only for individuals, but also for our families, communities and world. Forgiveness brings healing. Hatred only brings more strife.

Reflection: "But I tell you who hear me: Love your enemies, do good to those who hate you, bless those who curse you, pray for those who mistreat you" (Luke 6:27–28).

20

Who Are Our Gods?

Idolatry in the Modern World

We who live in the modern world would like to think that idolatry belongs to the ancient world of superstition. But idolatry is also part of the modern world. Anyone or anything other than God in which we put our hope and trust is an idol.

An often naive arrogance characterizes those who live in the twenty-first century, particularly those in the West. They appear to be secure in their self-sufficiency. They are proud of their technologies. They are convinced of their relativism. And they believe that they have left behind the world of ideologies.

These citizens of postmodernity have embraced a post-religious world. They believe that this new world leaves behind an era marked by zeal that leads to blindness, by faith that leads to bigotry, and by trust in God that leads to dependency. And so their logic goes, if you believe in nothing religious then idolatry is no longer possible. Practical atheism eliminates every idol.

If only it were all that simple. Karl Barth once made the observation that the human person is an idol-making factory. And Martin Luther King makes the observation that "we have relied on gods rather than God."[20] A skepticism about the God of the Bible does not eliminate the possibility that we create our own gods.

And we do just that! Westerners have their gods: individualism, consumerism, hedonism, scientism, militarism, just to mention a few. Of course, we would never call these "gods." How embarrassing that would be!

And to add further embarrassment, the New Testament counsels us as follows: "Put to death, therefore, whatever belongs to your earthly nature: sexual immorality, impurity, lust, evil desires and greed, which is idolatry" (Colossians 3:5).

In the West, we may want to hide behind our sophistication, where we simply rename and recast what does not suit us. But if our trust is not in the living God who has revealed himself in Jesus Christ through the Holy Spirit, it will be in something else. And, ironically, that something else even includes the denial of our idols. Trust in the denial does not make the idols go away.

Of course, idols are of our making. How foolish to trust what is simply under our control!

Reflection: "Declare what is to be, present it—let them take counsel together. Who foretold this long ago, who declared it from the distant past? Was it not I, the Lord? And there is no God apart from me, a righteous God and a Savior; there is none but me" (Isaiah 45:21).

21

Head and Heart

The Shaping of Mind and Spirit

So often the one is played off against the other: Tenderhearted people are softies and have no brain. Tough-minded people are ruthless and have no feeling and compassion. These are false dichotomies. One can have a sharp mind and be capable of making tough decisions, while at the same time be empathetic and caring.

Sometimes being a Christian is cast in terms of sentimentalism, and the impression is given that one has to throw one's mind away to be a Christian. But this is a serious misunderstanding of the Christian faith. We are not only to love God with our whole heart; we are also invited to think God's thoughts after him and to think about the whole of life in the light of faith. As such, our faith is one that seeks understanding.

We not only want to think seriously about our faith, we also seek to be tenderhearted toward God. We desire to live in God's presence with a loving and open posture. And here all the spiritual disciplines of prayer, solitude and meditation come into play.

But what we desire in our relationship with God is also what we seek to be in our attitude toward others, whether they be family, friend, neighbor, or stranger. As we think about others—and particularly about life in our world with its blessings and idolatries, with its joys and fears, and with its generosity and injustice—then we need a tough mind and a tender heart.

What a challenge it is for us to seek to make sense of our world with all its complexity and change. And furthermore, how are we to think about our world in the light of God's kingdom and God's desire to mend all creation and heal the nations? Hard theological thinking has not only God in view but also our world. And this thinking must give way to fervent prayer and to compassionate action.

We are to give our heart and mind to God in worship. We are called to give mind and heart to others in service. Martin Luther King summarized this well: "We must not stop with the cultivation of a tough mind. The Gospel also demands a tender heart."[21]

> *Reflection: "And we pray this in order that you may live a life worthy of the Lord and may please him in every way: bearing fruit in every good work, growing in the knowledge of God" (Colossians 1:10).*

22

Love

Its Painful and Joyous Transformation

Love is the most generous force in the universe. Love brought our world into being, and love alone can create and maintain a social order where life is lived to the full in the worship of God and the well-being of the other.

The God of the Bible is not some lonely monad hidden in the depths of the galaxy. And this God did not create the world full of creatures in order to meet his need for companionship and adulation. The God of the Bible is Trinity existing in a communion of love as Father, Son and Holy Spirit. It is out of this communion of love that God created all things.

The great miracle of the Christian life is that through the salvific work of Christ in the power of the Holy Spirit we are called into the communion and fellowship of the Trinity. Born out of the love of God, we are called into the love of the community of the Father, Son and Holy Spirit.

Martin Luther King once made the observation, "*Agape* . . . is an overflowing love. . . . It is not set in motion by any quality or function of its object. It is the love of God operating in the human heart."[22] Thus the love God has for humanity is the love we are to receive and celebrate and live out of. It is also the love we are to extend toward others.

This overflowing love is not a love only for our own. Because the love of God knows no boundaries and does not discriminate, so our love cannot simply be love of family and country. It also has to be love of other, love of stranger, love of enemy.

This love as overflow of the love God has for us is the love of welcome and service. It is a love that leads to table fellowship in the practice of hospitality. This is not a love of distance, but one of embracing. It is a love that breaks down all barriers and builds community.

Reflection: "And hope does not disappoint us, because God has poured out his love into our hearts by the Holy Spirit, whom he has given us" (Romans 5:5).

23

I Have a Dream

Looking to the Far Horizon

In any age there will be a majority who are the quiet and diligent maintainers of the social and institutional order. But there also will be some who are the visionaries, who can see new possibilities and who call for change.

Martin Luther King believed that the seemingly impossible was possible. And he proclaimed the dream and hope "that one day men [and women] will rise up and come to see that they were made to live together as brothers [and sisters]."[23] This vision was not simply one of racial integration and harmony. It was also a vision of economic sharing. And furthermore, it was a vision not simply of social goodwill but of genuine care and solidarity.

In one sense, this was a vision that extended the Christian ideal of love in the community of faith, the earthly body of Christ, to the wider society. It's a hope that suggests that all of us are meant to live in harmony and for the mutual well-being of the other.

In every way this is an impossible dream. It is also an eschatological one. It is in the new heavens and new earth that this impossible dream will be fully realized. There we will see the healing of the nations and swords finally beaten into ploughshares. In that new reality, there will be no more war, suffering and death.

But this impossible dream is one that we may all anticipate. It's a dream that we may pull out of the future, out of the heavens, to make it our own in our unjust and war-mongering world.

Christian hope is not simply premised on what God has done in Christ through the Holy Spirit. Christian hope also anticipates the future. We pray that what one day will be fully true will become true in our time in ever-greater ways.

In the human heart touched by the grace of the God who loves, redeems and makes whole, is the melody of King's dream. May our prayer for the inbreaking of God's kingdom lead us to dreaming and to action and service.

Reflection: "Seek good, not evil, that you may live. Then the LORD God Almighty will be with you, just as you say he is. Hate evil, love good; maintain justice in the courts" (Amos 5:14–15).

24

Healing the Community of Faith

The Church and Its Own Transformations

The church is called to be a community of forgiveness, healing and service to the world. But what it seeks to be for the world must be true of its own inner life. Hence the church itself must be continually converted and transformed.

The church in our contemporary world is going through one of its most difficult periods. This is particularly so in the Western world, where since the collapse of Christendom, the church has not only become marginalized, it is also held in disrepute. The mocking words unfairly hurled at Jesus on the cross ("you saved others; now save yourself") are with some justification now hurled at the church ("you want to save others; you'd better first save yourselves").

The scandal of the cross of Christ is the mystery of faith. In Christ's death new life has been won for all. The scandal of the church is no mystery of faith. It is the humiliation of the church listening to the hope of the church's own transformation and renewal.

Martin Luther King rightly reminds us that "when the church is true to its nature, it knows neither division nor disunity."[24] Much more could be said about the church when it lives in the grace of God and the power of the Spirit. Such a community of faith will be a people of worship, a people of learning, a people of fellowship, a people of nurture and care, and a people that seeks to wash the feet of the world.

But the church as a community of broken people can never be of itself all that it is meant to be. Of itself it cannot live up to such ideals, to such a high calling. The only way forward for the church is to live more fully in the communion of the Trinity; to live more fully in the grace of God; to live more truly led by the winsome Holy Spirit. In prayer we can only cry out, "Lord, heal us so that we may become a blessing to others."

Reflection: "All the believers were one in heart and mind. No one claimed that any of his possessions was his own, but they shared everything they had. With great power the apostles continued to testify to the resurrection of the Lord Jesus, and much grace was upon them all" (Acts 4:32–33).

25

The Power of Hope

LIVING THE POSSIBILITY OF THE IMPOSSIBLE

It is possible to be uncaring. It is also possible to be cynical. But we are most fully human when we live in hope. And we are most truly Christian when we live in the power of the hope of God's grace and healing in our midst.

It is, of course, possible to hope in anything and everything. And much of this may be mere wishful thinking. But when we hope for what is significant, it tells us something about ourselves. What we hope for reflects what we value.

For Christians, hope is to be grounded in the God who has revealed himself in Scripture and who continues to be with his people through the presence of the Holy Spirit. For them, hope does not lie in favorable cultural circumstances, in an upbeat economy, or in the power of politics. In fact, Christian hope can well up like subterranean waters in the most desolate of historical periods and places. It comes from a very different place than the favorable and pleasant winds of circumstance. Christian hope comes from faith. Faith in the God of Abraham, Isaac and Jacob, who has fully revealed himself in his Son, Jesus Christ. Faith in the Creator and Redeemer God, who out of love calls us into his life and into his service.

Martin Luther King once made the observation, "We must accept finite disappointment, but we must never lose infinite hope."[25] This does not mean that *our* hope is infinite. We are not that gallant and faithful. But hope as God's gift to the human heart, a gift that is given again and again, is a blessing we must never lose.

In other words, we may live in hope no matter how desolate the circumstances or how many the setbacks. We can continue to live in hope because we trust God to make a way, to part the waters, to open the heavens and to make the crooked places straight.

Reflection: "Then I said to them, 'You see the trouble we are in: Jerusalem lies in ruins, and its gates have been burned with fire. Come, let us rebuild the wall of Jerusalem, and we will no longer be in disgrace'" (Nehemiah 2:17).

26

Like the Master

Reflecting the Life of Christ in Our Conflicted World

The way of Christ was not the way of grandeur and power. It was the way of love, obedience, suffering and service. Christ came to heal humanity. When we walk the way of Christ, we too will be reconcilers and peacemakers.

Martin Luther King once reflected on the fact that the many awards that he had won, including the Nobel Peace Prize, were not that important. What was more important to him was that he had been a faithful servant of Jesus Christ. He stated, "If I can spread the message as the master [Jesus] taught, then my living will not be in vain."[26] This is a central vision that every Christian can embrace. What is most important is not fame or fortune, but bringing glory to God in our love and service to God and to our fractured world.

Reflecting the life of Christ in our conflicted world is no easy matter. We are constantly pressured to accept a dull conformity. We are expected to affirm the status quo. Those in power do not wish anyone to rock the boat. But to live for Christ, to live the way of Christ and to speak for Christ is to become a disturbing as well as a healing presence in our world. For it is the way of Christ that calls so many of the dominant values of our culture into question.

The way of Christ is to make God rather than ourselves the center of life. The way of Christ invites us to the path of forgiveness rather than to pursuing hatred and retaliation. The way of Christ invites us to build friendship and community rather than embrace the way of individualism. The way of Christ calls us to serve others rather than to think only of ourselves.

To be the servants of Christ and to bring Christ's message to the world is to call others to faith, to prayer, to forgiveness, to reconciliation and to peacemaking. To walk this way is to walk the way of faith, suffering and servanthood. It is certainly to walk the way of some sort of death in which we abandon our way and embrace the way of God's kingdom.

Reflection: "To this you were called, because Christ suffered for you, leaving you an example, that you should follow in his steps" (1 Peter 2:21).

27

Invitation

Called to Participate in the Grace of God

We are called to many things: work and play, responsibility and freedom, hardship and rejoicing. But the most basic, and yet most transformative, of all callings is to respond to God's invitation to friendship, forgiveness, and grace.

There are periods in history when all seems to be going well. This is the time for optimism. And this is when we think kindly of ourselves. At other times things are very different. Dark clouds gather over our social landscape. This is the time of anxiety and fear. This is the time when we may become despairing.

Theologically, we also see the swing of the pendulum. Humankind is good, we say. And so we celebrate freedom. At other times we think of the human being as bad, even demonic. And so we cry out for solutions and for deliverance.

In the pages of the biblical story, however, we read something very different. There the human person is depicted as *always* needing the love, forgiveness and grace of God. What is most surprising about the Bible's depiction of the human condition is that it is not only "bad" people who need the grace of God. "Good" people also need God's forgiveness. In fact, they sometimes need the grace of God more because, in the prowess of their own "goodness," they are more lost than ever.

Martin Luther King says it most simply: The human being "is a sinner in need of God's divine grace."[27] So whether one is a murderer or a millionaire, a pastor or a politician, a lawyer or a lawless person, a sinner or a saint, all need God's transforming love. This means that all need to come to the place of the greatest humility. The place where one can say, "It matters not what great things I have achieved; my greatest need is the forgiving grace of God." Or, "It matters not how badly I have failed and ruined my life and the lives of others; I can still come to the God of all mercy and grace." The greatest philosopher and the lowliest street person become one in repentance at the cross of Christ.

Reflection: "For all have sinned and fall short of the glory of God, and are justified freely by his grace through the redemption that came by Christ Jesus" (Romans 3:23–24).

28

The Greatest Gift

The Giving of Oneself

In the Western world we live with great generosity. We give to the poor and we give to the Third World. But our very giving is poor. It is marked by guilt. We have taken too much and our generous giving will never assuage our guilt.

There is little doubt that Martin Luther King gave himself to some of the most pressing causes of his time. These included not only the issue of racial injustice, but also the reality of war and the deep scar of poverty in a society of plenty. He was killed in the persistent pursuit of solutions for these grand anomalies in the social landscape of his time.

Therefore, King has some moral right to challenge us. He comments that people "give dollars to a worthwhile charity, but [they] give not of [their] spirit."[28] In other words, they don't give of themselves. They merely give materially and from their abundance.

Some readers may well say, What is wrong with that? It is giving *something!* Of course, this is true. It is giving something. But this kind of giving may be a little too close to what happens in many contemporary families. Two busy spouses in full-time careers can give little time to their children, but they can give much materially. To put this on a bigger social scale: We want the benefits of a grandiose lifestyle, and we are willing to give something to the poor. And to put this on a global scale: We are willing to give some aid to the Third World while we continue with our economic exploitation. In all these instances, this may be a form of giving that comes from wrongly gaining.

The giving of oneself is transformational and conversional giving. It is a giving against oneself and a giving for the sake of the other. In this giving I am no longer the center, but the other person is. This is the kind of giving that lies at the heart of the biblical story. God gives himself in Christ for the sake of the world. This is not giving something. This is giving all.

Reflection: "For even the Son of Man did not come to be served, but to serve, and to give his life as a ransom for many" (Mark 10:45).

29

Forgiveness

The Basic Rhythm of Life

Forgiveness cannot be the luxury that we sometimes extend to others like icing on the cake. Forgiveness is the glue of human relationality and sociality. Without it, our world would fall into chaos.

There are things in life we can change. With prayer, hard work, courage, love and hope, we can persistently labor for the transformation of relationships, settings and institutions. And thank God, much can and does change! But not everything changes. There are relationships that remain broken. There are institutions that continue in their powerful and exploitative ways. And much in our world remains unjust. In fact, the gap between rich and poor ever widens.

It is in the face of nonresolution that anger and bitterness always become the temptation. It is in the face of the persistence of evil that despair wants to move to center stage. And it is in the continuance of broken relationships that the temptation to doubt God's goodness and love becomes most pressing.

Martin Luther King knew something of the way in which power continues to benefit the powerful when it could be used to empower the poor. And he knew something of the reality of shattered dreams and a divided community. He is, therefore, right in reminding us that "forgiveness is not an occasional act; it is a permanent attitude."[29]

To live in a state of forgiveness, however, does not mean capitulation to the acts of wrongdoers. True forgiveness resists evil. It calls the victim to freedom from hatred and it calls the perpetrator to repentance. Forgiveness does not say, "It does not matter." It does not say, "That was not wrong." Forgiveness says, "It does matter. It matters so much that I am calling you to a new way, to change and transformation so that my forgiveness no longer becomes necessary."

Reflection: "Be merciful, just as your Father is merciful" (Luke 6:36).

30

Questing for Justice

The Search for Final Transformation

There are probably people in the world who are quite happy with the way things are. But they would have to be the secure and well-to-do. No one experiencing oppression, poverty, or marginalization is happy with the way things are. They want to see change.

Martin Luther King may well have been an optimist, but I think he was much more a person who lived out of a biblical vision. And as such we can make sense of his statement, "I am convinced that we shall overcome because the arc of the universe is long, but it bends toward justice."[30] A statement such as this can be based on the inevitability of historical necessity, but it can also refer to God's providential work in the world.

Humans have been given freedom and responsibility. But freedom can be abused and responsibility may be neglected. And thus again and again pain is propagated in the human community through neglect or oppression. There have been times in human history when the story of pain has been a seemingly never-ending story. It seemed so for the Hebrew slaves in Egypt. But deliverance did eventually come. And it is in this hope that we may live today. The God of the Bible still hears the cry of the poor and the vulnerable ones of the earth. And deliverance and healing will come.

But does it come quickly? This appears not to be the case.

Does it come fully? This also seems far away. The Hebrew slaves may have left Egypt, but Egypt had not left them; much of Egypt was still in their hearts.

The arc of justice as the fruit of God's grace may shed its blessings on a broken world. In these blessings we rejoice. But we also live tenaciously toward a future when all will be well. The vision for justice is finally an eschatological hope in the healing and mending of all creation. And in the meantime we cry out, pray and work for more of that future to become present.

Reflection: "There will no more death or mourning or crying or pain, for the old order of things has passed away" (Revelation 21:4).

31

Human Limitation

The Call to Cooperation

In the human community as well as in the church, significant leaders may emerge. These women and men challenge us to rethink the accepted and familiar and call us forward on the road to change and transformation. But great leaders also know their limitations and must live in great humility.

Becoming a great leader is usually the result of a confluence of factors: personal giftedness, a visionary orientation, courage, the crises of the times and the mobilization of others. Even this list of elements is by no means exhaustive. And the question will always remain whether great leaders are born or are made in the challenges of their times.

Great leaders, however, are not only characterized by ability and wisdom, but also by humility. Therefore Martin Luther King is right: "None of us can pretend that he [or she] knows all the answers."[31] This is so in every arena of life, whether it be politics, economics, religion, or the more direct areas of community organizing and working for social change.

We do our visioning, our planning and our strategizing. We mobilize people to achieve certain outcomes. But no matter how we plan and pray, we are at best seeing through a mirror darkly. As a consequence, great humility is always called for.

Hence, when vision leads to action, we are always called to

reflection. And reflection may well lead us to reevaluation and to refocusing. To be willing to adjust is a sign of humility. And sometimes a totally new direction needs to be set. This too is a form of death born out of humility.

That we don't have all the answers is the blessing that leads us to prayer. It is also the blessing that leads us to partnership and cooperation. If we think we know, but really don't, we are blinded. If we believe we know and are open to change and transformation, we, the wise, will walk the long road of renewal.

Reflection: "For this God is our God for ever and ever; he will be our guide even to the end" (Psalm 48:14).

32

Passionate

Carrying Convictions into Action

We sometimes give the impression that a Christian is nice and polite but finally a harmless creature. And with this comes the idea that a Christian should not be a radical. But of all people a Christian should be passionate in his or her love for the world.

Anyone who seeks to bring about significant change in family, neighborhood, institutions, church, or society is soon called into account. The most common way of attempting to bring about a halt in progress is to charge that the change agent or agents are going too fast, that they have to slow down, and that they are asking too much; they have to settle for less.

Other means are also used. Martin Luther King was also charged with being an extremist. The implication was that good Christians are not to be like that. They are to be polite and committed to the status quo. King's response was to redeem the term *extremist.* He asked, Was Jesus not an extremist in the cause of love? Was Amos not an extremist in the cause of justice? And, was Paul not an extremist for the Christian gospel? Then he concluded, "So the question is not whether we will be extremists, but what kind of extremists we will be. Will we be extremists for hate or for love?"[32]

This poses a particular challenge for us in our time. Christianity in the West has become a comfortable, middle-class, consumer Christianity. The church is passionate about neither the gospel nor the poor. Lacking a vision of the kingdom of God and failing to take seriously the Sermon on the Mount, the church in the West reflects the comfortableness of Western values rather than the values of the upside-down kingdom of God. Lacking prayer, it lacks passion. Lacking a vision of God, it lacks a vision of the neighbor in need. Lacking the experience of conversion, it lacks a vision of service.

Reflection: "May I never boast except in the cross of our Lord Jesus Christ, through which the world has been crucified to me, and I to the world. . . . Finally, let no one cause me trouble, for I bear on my body the marks of Jesus" (Galatians 6:14, 17).

33

The Power of the Cross

The Great Contradiction in History

The Cross tells us much about God, ourselves and our world. But its most powerful message is that it shows us the love of God in Christ in the redemption, transformation and healing of humanity.

Martin Luther King was adamant that the death of Christ is central to God's redemptive purpose for our world. He wrote, "There are some who still find the cross a stumbling block, and others consider it foolishness, but I am more convinced than ever before that it is the power of God unto social and individual salvation."[33]

This emphasis is an important challenge for us, for so often Christ's death on the cross is only linked to the matter of personal salvation. As evangelicals we are fond of saying, "Jesus died for me." And while this is true, we may lose sight of the width and scope of the salvation that Christ has brought about. Christ's death on the cross not only paves the way that *I* can be forgiven, but also opens the way of salvation to the whole of humanity. Christ carried the sins of the whole world "in his body on the tree" (1 Peter 2:24).

But the sacrificial death of Christ was not only to achieve new life for me, but also to bring into being the new humanity—the body of Christ. The community of faith where we all are brothers and sisters in Christ is the fruit of his work on the cross. This redeemed community, in which the barriers of race, gender and economic status are overcome, is the blessing that flows directly from the cross, for the salvation in Christ makes us new and makes us one.

The Cross was not only key to the life of Christ; it also is key to our lives as his followers. The cross of Christ has blessed us, but it also marks us. We too are to die to the ways of the world and to live wholly for God. We too are to give ourselves in sacrificial service to God for the sake of the world. Thus the Christian lives a cruciform existence. The Christian wants to live for others in the way that Christ lived and died for him or her.

Reflection: "We were therefore buried with him through baptism into death in order that, just as Christ was raised from the dead through the glory of the Father, we too may live a new life" (Romans 6:4).

34

God, Our Helper

Turning to the God Who Aids Us

In the most fundamental way, we are all wholly dependent on God, for we live and move and have our very being in the God who created us and who upholds us. But we are also dependent on God's grace and the Holy Spirit and on the special ways God helps us in times of difficulty and need.

It matters not what sphere of life we are talking about, whether it is family, work, science, economics, the arts, or politics, we all find ourselves in times of difficulty and need. Again and again life throws up its surprising problems, its seemingly unsolvable difficulties; the unexpected and even the tragic remain a part of the human condition.

While prayer is to be the rhythm of the whole of our lives, including in times of blessing and ease, and while prayer is primarily fellowship and friendship with God, it nevertheless is also sometimes the panicked heart cry. Martin Luther King spoke of such moments when at short notice he had to give an important speech on civil rights issues. He commented, "With nothing left but faith in a power whose matchless strength stands over against the frailties and inadequacies of human nature, I turned to God in prayer."[34]

This is the magic of Christian life and the beauty of our relationship with God the Father, the Son and the Holy Spirit.

God has promised to be with us always. In the joys of the birth of a child, in the happiness of a newfound job, in the security of a growing friendship, God's presence is there.

But also in the other movements and moments of life's experience, God has promised to be an ever-present help in times of trouble. In the moments of inadequacy, the times of despair, in situations of feeling overwhelmed, the God of all grace has promised to give us aid. While prayer can be like gentle murmurings among friends, it can also be the heart cry in times of insecurity and need.

In living this way, we reflect more truly the human condition that we are not self-sufficient and need God's grace and help.

Reflection: "To you I call, O Lord my Rock; do not turn a deaf ear to me. For if you remain silent, I will be like those who have gone down to the pit" (Psalm 28:1).

35

Self-Giving

Committed to a Cause Greater Than Ourselves

Real life is not living only for our own frequently narrow concerns. The vision that has only oneself in view is a vision that narrows the arteries of the heart of love. To truly live is to live for something greater, even though it may cost our all.

We can live in a whole variety of ways. This includes living without hope, direction, or purpose. But most of us seek to live for something or someone. Because we are meaning-making creatures, we seek to make sense of life and seek to live for some purpose.

For some this purpose is wholly altruistic. They live for the well-being and betterment of others. This was true for Martin Luther King, who said, "I choose to identify with the underprivileged. I choose to identify with the poor. . . . I choose to give my life for those who have been left out of the sunlight of opportunity."[35] To live like this requires a profound inner transformation. No one lives readily and helpfully for others unless a deep conversion has taken place. And no one lives for the poor unless he or she has been marked by the cross of Christ. Living for others in order to benefit and to empower them can only come from the blessing of someone else having lived for us.

God in Christ gave himself for us. So we too can give ourselves in love and service for others. Christ became the humiliated and suffering one. So we too, by his grace, can suffer with and for others. Christ gave himself in service to the poor. To them the good news of the kingdom of God was proclaimed. So we too, in walking in the footsteps of Christ and encouraged by his example, can give ourselves in serving the poor.

The greater our identification with Christ, the greater our Christlikeness and the greater our willingness to embrace the concerns of the reign of God to redeem, heal and renew all that is broken in our world.

Reflection: "Then he said to them all: 'If anyone would come after me, he must deny himself and take up his cross daily and follow me'" (Luke 9:23).

36

A Long Obedience

Committed to the Slow March of Justice

When major changes occur in our world, we hope that everything will now be different. We hoped that the end of World War II would end all wars. We hoped that modern economic prosperity would end world poverty. But whatever our hopes may have been, injustice continues in our world. And so we are called to a long obedience and to a life of suffering.

Repeatedly, in the strange and convoluted story of history, there come those moments when men and women cry out, "Enough is enough," and they seize the moment to call for change. There has been the cry to end slavery, the cry to end colonialism and the cry to end racial segregation.

There is also much that we can cry about today. Global poverty is but one moral intolerable that should bring us to our knees in prayer, should bring us into the streets in protest, should bring us into the Third World in committed and sacrificial service.

But neither the issues of the past nor those of the present are easily solved. Cheap and easy change is not what history teaches us. Martin Luther King is, therefore, to the point: "Every step toward the goal of justice requires sacrifice, suffering and struggle."[36]

Some causes are so big that a lifetime of commitment and

service is too short. So what does it take to walk the long road of obedience, identification and service? What does it take to cry until there are no more tears? Much is required. But the most basic is the call of God. God has called me to this task and so I can do no other. And I will fulfill this calling even if it costs me everything, even my life.

So often we make the intolerable tolerable. So often we accept things as the realities of our time. But where we have said yes, God has said no. And God's no is a yes to mercy, forgiveness, justice, peace, reconciliation and healing. It is God's yes that will fuel our obedience on the long road to justice.

Reflection: "Since my people are crushed, I am crushed; I mourn, and horror grips me. Is there no balm in Gilead? Is there no physician there? Why then is there no healing for the wounded of my people?" (Jeremiah 8:21–22).

37

I've Seen the Promised Land

Embracing an Eschatological Vision

There is much that can sustain us in the journey of faith, in the discipline of prayer and in a life of service. But finally it has to be more than idealism or pragmatism. Nothing can sustain us like a God-given vision.

There is little doubt that Martin Luther King was caught up in the larger forces of history as he championed racial integration, the relief of poverty, and as he campaigned against the war in Vietnam. But it is also clear that he had personally committed himself to these issues as a man called by God, and that he was willing to take upon himself the burden and suffering of these causes.

There is little doubt that all of this weighed heavily on him, that at times he felt overwhelmed, and that long-term solutions seemed far away. But toward the end of his life so tragically and prematurely snuffed out, something fundamentally changed. King had a vision that took him beyond the pressure of the issues he was fighting for. And it took him beyond fear. In one of his famous speeches he exclaimed: "[God has] allowed me to go up to the mountain. And I've looked over. And I've seen the promised land."[37] In this clear allusion to Moses before his death, King suggested that a similar fate may await him: death before the culmination of one's life work.

This is a freeing way to live. The cause is no longer the most important. One's own safety is no longer preeminent. But the eschatological vision takes center stage. This is the vision of what God will do with us or without us. This is the unraveling of God's final purpose against all doubt and all opposition, compromise and difficulty.

In this faith we may all live. God's kingdom of righteousness and shalom is breaking into our world and will finally come with such power that all things will be restored and made whole. In the light of this faith we can begin to live in relinquishment and surrender, because God will fulfill his purposes.

Reflection: "Then the LORD said to him, 'This is the land I promised on oath to Abraham, Isaac and Jacob when I said, "I will give it to your descendants."'" (Deuteronomy 34:4).

38

God and Prayer

When Prayer Is More Than Human Activity

We have dissected prayer into its many forms and expressions. But there is a great mystery to prayer. And synchronicity is one of the indicators of its mysterious nature. This occurs when the human heart cry and God's sovereign response meet.

Martin Luther King makes an important observation regarding prayer when he notes that "God both evokes and answers prayer."[38] We tend to think of God only as a prayer-answering God. After all, God is most powerful and most loving and generous, so God is desirous to answer our prayers and to extend his goodness and help toward us.

We readily acknowledge that there is a slight risk in this kind of thinking. This can make God a sort of cosmic Father Christmas who fulfills all our wishes and desires. We all know from experience that God does not always answer our prayers in the way we have hoped. And even in the way God answers prayer, there is mystery at work.

But King refers to the other, and often overlooked, dimension of prayer. Prayer is something that God through the Holy Spirit births and grows within us. One of the chief characteristics of renewal and revival movements is that people give themselves to prayer as never before. And those who testify to new infillings of the Holy Spirit speak of a renewal in their prayer life. It is as if something new is born within the heart through the Holy Spirit and this bubbles forth in praise and prayer.

When God is at work within us, inspiring us to pray, the mystery of synchronicity most readily occurs. I am led to pray for someone or something, and later I discover the relevance of those prayers. Therefore prayer is as much a gift as it is an activity. And being led to pray by the Holy Spirit reminds us of the great network of mutuality that constitutes being part of the community of faith and the purposes of God in our time.

Reflection: "Whom have I in heaven but you? And earth has nothing I desire besides you. My flesh and my heart may fail, but God is the strength of my heart and my portion forever" (Psalm 73:25–26).

39

Powerful yet Deprived

The Spiritual Emptiness of the West

The power of the West, particularly the United States, is awesome and inspiring. Almost everything is possible technologically and militarily. But this power has blinded us to the poverty of spirit and community that blights our inner world and our social landscape.

When you think about a great person, this person's material wealth is not the first thing that comes to mind. Greatness is usually thought of in terms of what the person has achieved. This can be in the field of music, art, philosophy, religion, or politics.

This should also be the way in which we think about a nation. Its greatness does not primarily lie in its national economic wealth, but in its cultural ethos, its creativity that uplifts the human spirit, its community and care, and its ability to empower the least in the society. Because this vision of a good and civil society is not always championed, it is necessary to become concerned as Martin Luther King was concerned about the society of his day when he wrote, "Spiritual power lags so far behind her [the United States'] technological abilities."[39]

This sad but true comment can be made about the West as a whole. The West is not known for its spirituality, and the church in the West is in many ways a culturally captive church. Therefore it is imperative that if national recovery is to occur, the Christian community must play a vital part. And this can take place only when the church itself undergoes a profound spiritual renewal.

Spiritual renewal is not simply moments of ecstasy. It is a transformation of heart and mind. It is being drawn into God's kingdom concerns and living in the power of the Spirit. Spiritual renewal has Christ at the center and involves ordering our lives to live Christ's way in the world. A church characterized by the *imitatio Christi* is a church that will lift up the soul of a nation.

Reflection: "The LORD will lay bare his holy arm in the sight of all the nations, and all the ends of earth will see the salvation of our God" (Isaiah 52:10).

40

Inner Strength

The Peace and Power God Alone Can Give

Life has its smooth waters and rough seas. Life has its joys and sorrows. And while we need God's presence, grace and empowerment in all the seasons of life, we especially need God to be with us in times of trouble.

Martin Luther King held a belief that should also characterize each one of us: "God is able to give us interior resources to confront the trials and difficulties of life."[40] There are some important dimensions embedded in this simple statement of faith in God's care and love.

While in the rough seas of life, though we may think we only need practical help, such as relief from our difficulties, we may also need other forms of help such as faith, perseverance and courage. These are important blessings as well. These gifts of grace strengthen us on the inside.

Living in a culture that is so materially oriented and so given to pragmatics, it is easy for us to overlook and not to use these inner spiritual resources that give us life, energy and hope. In difficult times we can easily become overwhelmed, reactive and angry. We can lose hope. We can fall into the pit of despair. Therefore it is so important that we be strengthened within through the work of the Holy Spirit, whose presence, gifts and graces we seek.

The other important element in King's belief is that, empowered from within, we can actively respond to the difficulties of life rather than deny, ignore, or evade them. It is easy to bury our head in the sand. It is also possible to give up. But inward blessings are for outward service. Inner graces are for washing the feet of the world. Spirituality is for mission. And the graces and blessings of God are also for and in the situation.

In the heat of conflict one may receive the gift of God's peace. In the moment of fear one may find courage. And in the darkness of despair, a candle of hope may be lit.

Reflection: "I pray also that the eyes of your heart may be enlightened in order that you may know the hope to which he has called you, the riches of his glorious inheritance in the saints, and his incomparably great power for us who believe" (Ephesians 1:18–19).

41

Vicarious Suffering

Carrying Others' Burdens and Shame

To love others truly is to be drawn not only into their goodness but also into their dysfunction, anger, pain and bigotry. This does not mean that we become like them, but it does mean that we are willing to carry some of their pain until it becomes transmuted into healing.

Both goodness and suffering lay at the very heart of the moral realities of the universe.

Goodness is at the heart of God's creative activity. It is also at the heart of God's providential care for the world. And goodness, however strong or weak, also lies at the heart of the social and moral fabric of our world. The goodness of love and care is what empowers our families and social institutions.

While God's goodness and beneficence are consistent and strong, our goodness is often fragile, inconsistent and weak. In fact, there are times when our goodness is darkness. It is the ungoodness of our goodness that opens up the dimensions of suffering.

God's response to human disobedience, sin and failure was to engage it creatively rather than to walk away. And God's ultimate engagement was to suffer himself, in Christ. God in Christ took upon himself the sin and shame of our ungoodness.

In some small way, we are invited to do the same. We too can take upon ourselves the failures and wrongdoings of members of our family and others. It is also possible to take upon ourselves the wrongdoing of a community or a society and to bear its shame, while at the same time seeking to bring about change and transformation. Martin Luther King sought to live this way. He said, "I have faith to believe that this excessive suffering that is now coming to our family will in some little way serve to make Atlanta a better city, Georgia a better state, and America a better country. . . . If I am correct then our suffering is not in vain."[41]

Reflection: "He himself bore our sins in his body on the tree so that we might die to sins and live for righteousness; by his wounds you have been healed" (1 Peter 2:24).

42

Resistance

In the Long March of Justice We Have to Say, No

Much religious language is the talk of love. It is also the talk of obedience. But religious language is also the language of protest. In the face of evil it is willing to say, no. And in the face of injustice it is willing to pray and work for a better way.

Sadly, so much of contemporary Western Christianity is characterized by blandness. Many Christians hold an inherent conservatism and are self-preoccupied. The larger issues of our world receive scant attention. And the themes of struggle, sacrifice and resistance are far from our daily praxis.

Therefore Martin Luther King is most relevant in this critical matter. He wrote, "The tendency of most is to adopt a view that is so ambiguous that it will include everything and so popular that it will include everybody." Pleasing everyone means that nothing ever changes. He goes on: "Many people fear nothing more terrible than to take a position which stands out sharply and clearly from the prevailing opinion."[42]

It is so easy in religious circles to mark this as the language of the radical, the rebel, or the revolutionary. And as such it is regarded as language that does not belong to the prayerful heart and to the worship in the sanctuary. But such a position fails to hear the liberating themes of the biblical story.

The whole prophetic tradition of the Old Testament is a very clear, no, to the prevailing attitudes and values of those in power in Israel. This tradition uplifts the voice of the poor, oppressed and victimized, and cries for repentance and justice. The words and work of Jesus embody a clear, no, to the Judaism of that time and celebrate the good news of the kingdom coming to the poor. It is this biblical story that is to shape, define and orient our posture in the contemporary world.

Christians shaped by the reign of God are aliens and strangers in this world. They are out of step with our culture's dominant values. Thus we need to embrace the pain of being different, but also embrace the suffering of praying and working for a changed world.

Reflection: "But as for me, I am filled with power, with the Spirit of the LORD, and with justice and might, to declare to Jacob his transgression, to Israel his sin" (Micah 3:8).

43

A Holistic Vision

Joining the Work of Charity and Justice

Christians are called to active participation in our world. This should never become reductionistic. Instead, all of life is to be lived to God's glory and to the well-being of others. Thus evangelism and social concern belong together. And serving the church as well as the wider community is part of our calling.

We can never say that a particular sphere of life is not our concern. We cannot say we will only be concerned with the soul condition of humanity and leave the social, political and economic realities to others and to the government. The reason we cannot live this way is that it goes against the major contours of the biblical narrative.

Yahweh, the covenant-making and redeeming God of the Old Testament, was concerned not only with the spiritual well-being of his people, but also with their social and economic conditions. The Old Testament prophets were not only concerned with temple purity and prayer, but also with a social vision of justice and provision for the poor.

In the mission of Jesus, word and deed belonged together. A wholeness of heart, but also a wholeness of community was central to Jesus' vision of the kingdom of God. Martin Luther King espoused a similar vision: "We are called to play the Good Samaritan on life's roadside, but that will be only an initial act.

. . . We must come to see that the whole Jericho road must be transformed so that men and women will not be constantly beaten and robbed as they make their journey on life's highway."[44]

It is obvious what King has in view. We are called to help individuals. We are also called to change social structures that bind and oppress people. The micro and macro levels both need to be infused and transformed by the love and grace of God. Thus the vision is not only good persons but also good institutions; not only good hearts but also good laws; not only the good work of rescue but also the good work of social transformation. While being a good Samaritan is a momentary act of charity, the work of justice is the long journey of working for change.

Reflection: "They will rebuild the ancient ruins and restore the places long devastated; they will renew the ruined cities that have been devastated for generations" (Isaiah 61:4).

44

Divine Initiative, Human Cooperation

The Dance of the Divine-Human Partnership

We are not God. Nor are we nothing. We are not sinless. Nor are we without some goodness. We cannot save ourselves, but God uses us to save others. God is sovereign, but God chooses to link himself to human obedience and cooperation.

There is a great mystery in understanding ourselves and in understanding the being and ways of God. But there is an even greater mystery in understanding humanity's relationship with God.

In Christ, through the Holy Spirit, we are invited and drawn into the fellowship and love and community of the Trinity. And in the mystery of faith, God dwells with us through the Spirit. In the joy and dynamics of this relationship, which ever grows and deepens, we do not become divine but become ever conformed to the likeness of Christ and grow in awareness of God's presence and love. Not only do we not become divine, but we remain fallible, vulnerable and in need of God's forgiveness, renewal and healing. And yet God wants to use us for his purposes. He wants us to be a sign, sacrament and servant of the reign of God.

King is careful to spell out possible misunderstandings in this divine-human relationship as he writes, "The real weakness of the idea that God will do everything is its false conception of both God and [humans]. It makes God so absolutely sovereign that [the human] is absolutely helpless. It makes [the human] so absolutely depraved that he [or she] can do nothing but wait for God."[44]

The domain for divine-human cooperation, however, needs to be carefully identified. It does not lie in the realm of salvation. We don't cooperate with God in bringing about our salvation. God alone in Christ has gained redemption for us. Instead, this cooperation lies in the service of God. We are invited to join with God in his salvific purposes for our world. So we are invited to pray. We are called to witness. We are called to raise a prophetic voice. We are invited to be instruments of healing. And we are called to the work of justice. This cooperation, however, is always working with God through the power of the Spirit.

Reflection: "We are therefore Christ's ambassadors, as though God were making his appeal through us" (2 Corinthians 5:20).

45

Prayer and Work

The Dynamics of Their Interrelationship

Our contemporary world is not that interested in whether a person prays or not. It is more interested in that one works. After all, productivity is a dominant theme in our culture. Sadly, it is not too much different in the church in the West. Prayer is held in poor regard in relation to service.

While there are small sections of the contemporary church in the West that hold a world-denying form of Christianity and are therefore inner-focused, most churches are the opposite. There is a strong commitment to many forms of activism.

Activism is good. There is much to be done in our broken and unjust world. And Christians have a wonderful opportunity through their loving service to others to mirror the great love God has for all humanity, including the poor. But activism can also be a trap. One can be tempted to do much and lose oneself in much doing. As a result, work becomes much more important than prayer.

Instead, we want to celebrate both activism and prayer as central. But are they related, and if so, in what way? Martin Luther King highlights both dimensions of the relationship: "I take prayer too seriously to use it as an excuse for avoiding work and responsibility."[45] Not only are there times when we must act, there are also times when we must pray. Just as prayer can be used as an excuse not to take a stand (because I have to pray more about it), so work can be used as an excuse not to pray (there is so much that needs to be done and so few to do it). Thus one of the corrective things one can say is, "I take my work and service so seriously that I commit myself to fervent prayer."

This reflection brings us to a most basic realization: Externalization through what I do is related to internalization. My inner and outer worlds are to be connected. Contemplation and action belong together, as do prayer and service, and solitude and community. And God's sovereignty and human responsibility are all part of an invisible web of connectedness.

Do much! But pray much also!

Reflection: "If one of you says to him, 'Go, I wish you well; keep warm and well fed,' but does nothing about his physical needs, what good is it? In the same way, faith by itself, if it is not accompanied by action, is dead" (James 2:16–17).

46

This World

The Inbreaking of God's Reign

According to the biblical record, there will be a future when all things will be made whole. But the blessings of God are not only for a future time. They are also for the here and now. Grace, forgiveness, healing, community and the impact of God's goodness on the world are everywhere to be seen. But we pray and work for more of God's reign to break in and transform us.

One of the sad themes of colonial Christianity was the idea that oppressed indigenous peoples impacted by the gospel should not support political change efforts. They should be content that Christ had changed their hearts. And since heaven awaits them, they should be patient regarding reforms in the present.

Martin Luther King also encountered this kind of thinking during the efforts to achieve racial equality for African-Americans. He commented, "It's all right to talk about 'silver slippers over yonder' but men [and women] need shoes to wear down here."[46]

What is so curious about the idea that certain Christians, particularly the oppressed, should be accepting of their lot in life is that this notion is not consistently applied to all. For example, we don't say this to middle-class Christians who are working seventy hours a week and have both father and mother in the workplace. We don't say to them, "Work less and accept your economic circumstances." We do the opposite. We laud their commitment to industriousness and hard work.

So if the middle class can improve its lot, why should the poor not do so? The difference, of course, is that the poor call for fundamental change while others support the way things are.

In the frame of God's reign, the least must be in view. The Bible has the poor and oppressed in view. And Scripture calls for service to the poor as a sign of service and love for God himself.

The good news of the kingdom of God is not only for the future. It is also for now, and it is also for the poor.

Reflection: "So he replied to the messengers, 'Go back and report to John what you have seen and heard: The blind receive sight, the lame walk, those who have leprosy are cured, the deaf hear, the dead are raised, and the good news is preached to the poor'" (Luke 7:22).

47

In Our Time

Seeing God's Hand in Human Affairs

The works of God are not evident only in nature or only in the church; they are also to be seen in social and political movements. However, to see the finger of God in human affairs is much more difficult and calls for careful discernment. But God is at work in our world, working out his purposes through human endeavors.

Martin Luther King operated on the premise that the movement toward racial integration was not simply a sociopolitical movement. It was also a movement in which God by his Spirit was at work. And so he could exclaim, "I'm just happy that God has allowed me to live in this period, to see what is unfolding because I see God working."[47]

Maybe in times of significant change we too can have that sort of confidence that God is at work in our world. But often this doesn't seem to be the case when life, in its ordinariness, meanders on. We may sense that God is at work in our hearts. We may experience God in the sanctuary in times of worship, sacrament, or preaching. But where is God in our general society and in the economic and political realities of our world? These dimensions of life seem to be so devoid of God's grace and justice!

But before we dismiss God too quickly from the human and social arena, we need to engage in some careful reflection. Is the goodness in our world simply the product of human effort? Is the persistent struggle for justice in a world of poverty and oppression simply the fruit of human concern? One could go on asking these and similar questions. Despite the difficulties in our world, there are ongoing impulses for good. So where do these come from?

I join with King to suggest that God is at work in our world. God's Spirit is brooding over our social world as much as the Spirit was hovering over the initial chaos of the primal world. Thus in any age there are the signs of the Spirit at work upholding and mending God's world. For this vision we need to have eyes of faith and a heart full of hope and love.

Reflection: "For the sake of Jacob my servant, of Israel my chosen, I summon you [Cyrus] by name and bestow on you a title of honor, though you do not acknowledge me. . . . I will give you the treasures of darkness" (Isaiah 45:4, 3).

48

Dissent

Raising a Prophetic Voice

We live in difficult and complex times. As a result, we are ever ready to listen to those in authority. But while these authorities may be right, they may also at times be wrong. If the God of the Old Testament raised up prophets to challenge the God-appointed kingship, then we should not be surprised that prophets need to be raised up in our day.

Dissent is not a favorite word in the community of faith. Love and unity are. Nor is the church's role as a dissenting voice in the wider society one that the church relishes. The opposite is in fact the case. The church sees itself more as a peacemaker and healer in society than as a prophetic voice.

And yet the church, if it is true to its very nature, cannot but be such a voice. Martin Luther King locates the need for this prophetic activity in the circumstances in which the church finds itself: "During these days of human travail we must encourage creative dissenters. We need them because the thunder of their fearless voices will be the only sound stronger than the blasts of bombs and the clamor of war hysteria."[48]

It is appropriate to locate prophetic activity in one's setting. But it is more basic to locate it in the very nature of who God is and in the scope of God's action among us—in other words, to give prophecy a theological center.

It is in Christ that we can most clearly see God's prophetic activity. Jesus as servant of the reign of God called religious leaders to repentance, walked the road of the peaceable kingdom, blessed the poor and calls us to follow in his footsteps. To follow Christ is a form of prophecy. To live his gospel in the power of the Spirit is the way of prophecy.

The way of Christ is very different from the way of the contemporary world, with its use of power, control, production and functional values. Thus prophecy is not primarily a reaction to our world but the outworking of our commitment to Christ. As such, because of Christ we say no to the madness of our world.

Reflection: "To whom can I speak and give warning? Who will listen to me? Their ears are closed so they cannot hear. The word of the LORD is offensive to them; they find no pleasure in it" (Jeremiah 6:10).

49

God with Us

God in the Arena of Life

The God of the Bible is both transcendent and immanent. God is both wholly other and wholly concerned. God enters the human fray and at the same time remains the God whom the highest heavens cannot contain. God joins himself to our lives and our concerns but remains the Other who calls us into his purposes.

In one of his sermons, Martin Luther King lauds the closeness and attentiveness of God, proclaiming, "God is at work in his universe. He is not outside the world looking on with a sort of cold indifference. Here on all the roads of life, he is striving in our striving."[49] It is true that God does not dwell in holy isolation in the heavens. The God of the Bible has come among us, most closely in Christ. And God's coming among us is not one of mere observation but one of redemptive suffering and transformational activity.

But God's relationship to our activity is more complex than King indicates. God both joins us and asks us to join him. God identifies with us but also challenges us. God is for us, but God is also against us, even though in his againstness he is for us.

What all of this means is that God never fully endorses the work of our hands. The work of preaching or prophecy, the work of evangelism or social justice, the work of homemaking or politics can all be done to the glory of God and to human betterment. And in that work we can seek God's direction and blessing. But this work will always be *our* work. And as such it is subject to sin, failure and correction. Thus, while God is in our striving, he is also against our striving.

God's kingdom way is never fully our way; therefore we are called to repentance in our service to God and humanity. This calls for great humility. It is very convenient for us to proclaim that God is with us and that God is on our side. But it is a more accurate picture to confess that we *trust* that God is with us while we recognize that God also challenges us and calls us to an ever-deeper conversion.

Reflection: "We wait in hope for the Lord; he is our help and our shield. In him our hearts rejoice, for we trust in his holy name. May your unfailing love rest upon us, O Lord, even as we put our hope in you" (Psalm 33:20–22).

50

God's Call

Responding to God's Way for Us

The framework of God's will does not need to be discovered. It has been revealed and recorded in Scripture and therefore needs to be understood and embraced. But what God calls us to vocationally needs to be discerned. This opens up the dynamic dance of God's call and our human response.

When Martin Luther King was reflecting on his call to the ministry, he said that the call "came neither by some miraculous vision nor by some blinding light. . . . [It] gradually came upon me."[50] Many of us can relate to this and can echo similar sentiments. Many of our big decisions made carefully and prayerfully were not the product of some cataclysmic unveiling. These decisions were the result of a gradual unfolding.

What is even more remarkable in all of this is that God's call is not something that boxes us in. The call is not static. It is dynamic. It is not a call that circumscribes us. It liberates us.

The way in which God calls us, however, is a sign that God is with us in special but also in the most ordinary of ways. God can work through our family upbringing, our education, our context and our personality. God can also work sovereignly and dramatically.

This more ordinary work of God is also a work of his grace and goodness. In fact, it is a dramatic work, for God makes his way and will for us known through the long process of personal formation. When we look back on all of this, we are amazed. How remarkable that God already laid the foundation of this call in my family of origin, in my being parented, in my schooling and upbringing! How amazing that God was already at work then!

To recognize this way of God with us is to acknowledge God's sovereignty and lordship. God doesn't call us in a vacuum. Rather, he has been at work in time and events, preparing us for the call to come.

Reflection: "You know when I sit and when I rise; you perceive my thoughts from afar. You discern my going out and my lying down; you are familiar with all my ways" (Psalm 139:2–3).

51

Loved by God

Bearing the Marks of God's Creation

There are many different ways by which we may seek to understand the human being. Biology, sociology and psychology give us windows into the mystery that we are. But the biblical story gives us the most foundational insight: We are creatures made in God's image and are loved and cherished by God.

The long history of humanity is replete not only with examples of exemplary love and care extended to family, friend and foe, but also with examples of a demeaning inhumanity to others. Certain groups of people have always been marginalized and victimized in society. And in our more personal relationships with one another there are examples of neglect or even abuse.

There are many reasons we should not behave toward another person in this way. But the most basic reason is theological. King has carefully pointed this out. He writes: "The important thing about the [human being] is . . . not the texture of [one's] hair or the color of [one's] skin but his [or her] eternal worth to God."[51] This perspective has important implications. To treat another human being in a demeaning way—or to marginalize another because he or she is different—is to insult the value that God places on that person. Each person is precious in God's sight; therefore, we should treat that person with a love that reflects the love of God.

True love of God involves a love of neighbor, and this leads to an end of racism and discrimination. Sadly, the Christian community has not always been characterized by the generous arc of God's love. Love of one's family or group or even nation has taken priority over an indiscriminate love for all. Thus King's words challenge us. All persons are of eternal worth to God. All are made in God's image. That includes those whom dominant society ignores, neglects, or rejects.

Reflection: "For you created my inmost being; you knit me together in my mother's womb. I praise you because I am fearfully and wonderfully made; your works are wonderful, I know that full well" (Psalm 139:13–14).

52

God's Presence

The God of All Our Journeys

We are sometimes tempted to think that the God of the Bible is only the God of favorable weather conditions. These circumstances, we think, are the sign of God's presence and care. But God is as much, if not more so, the One who makes himself present in the storm and darkness.

There are some Christians who live a life of second-guessing. They are always wondering if they are still okay with God. And they use various indicators to try to determine this. So when things are going well, God is smiling on them. When things are difficult, they must have done something wrong and God must be displeased. Trying to live within this overly simplistic schema is a nightmare. It is also a wrong way of looking at life. And more fundamentally, it is a wrong way of understanding God's way with us.

God does not run hot or cold with us depending on our performance or spirituality. That is what *we* do to each other in unhealthy relationships. Some of us may have grown up in families where we were loved because we were good. Or we may be in adult relationships now that are performance based. But these scenarios are not cameos of God's way with us. God loved us while we were sinners. And God continues to love us in our strengths and weaknesses, in our victories and brokenness.

Martin Luther King has put this well. He exclaimed, "We may be consoled that God has two lights: a light to guide us in the brightness of the day when hopes are fulfilled and circumstances are favorable, and a light to guide us in the darkness of the midnight when . . . the slumbering giants of gloom and hopelessness rise in our souls."[32]

We may put this even stronger: God himself is with us in our brightest hour and in our darkest moment. In the dance of joy and in the dirge of suffering, God can be found. But we need the eyes of faith for both. In joy we can neglect God, and in suffering we can complain, but God is there in all the contours and journeys of life.

Reflection: "I was young and now I am old,
yet I have never seen the righteous forsaken"
(Psalm 37:25).

53

Procrastination

Failing to Seize the Day

We are mostly so busy with life that we don't have the time or the energy to ask the larger questions about our life's direction and purpose. Much less do we have the space to think about the larger issues of society's shape, values and preoccupations. And because these reflections are inadequate we often don't know what to say or how to act. And so we procrastinate.

One of the worrying realities of our time is that we appear to be less and less confident that we know what is really happening in our society and in our world. We are also less confident that we can change anything. Government, institutions and major corporations are just too big for us to understand, let alone to confront about matters of injustice.

As a result, we may vaguely hope that things will get better, but we are basically resigned to the way things are. And we feel that we can act less and less in response to wider and broader social issues. We feel that we can't change things in our places of work, let alone in the wider society. And even when we feel uneasy or concerned about the way some things are, we often don't know how to respond. Because we have no companions in our concerns, we feel alone and fail to act. Martin Luther King speaks about "procrastination . . . [as] the thief of time." He goes on to say, "Life often leaves us standing bare, naked and dejected with a lost opportunity."[53]

What all of this suggests to us is that we need to read the signs of the times, we need companions on the journey, and we need strategies for seeking to bring about change. But we don't need to know everything. What we do need is courage. We need to seize the day.

None of this effort can be action without prayer, doing without discernment, service without contemplation. Nor can it merely be hoping and wishful thinking. To bring about change we must act. And the best action is symbolic and prophetic. But for this unusual action, we must look to God and wait on him for insight.

Reflection: "Then break the jar while those who go with you are watching, and say to them, 'This is what the LORD Almighty says: I will smash this nation and this city just as this potter's jar is smashed and cannot be repaired'" (Jeremiah 19:10–11).

54

Worship

Entering the Dance of Celebration

However strange this may seem to some, the heart of Christianity is not first of all word, sacrament, or service, but worship. In worship we gaze on the Creator and Redeemer in love and gratitude and celebrate the grace of God and the reign of God. At the heart of the Christian story is the dance of celebration.

Despite advances in the modernity project, our world is still characterized by instrumental reason, pragmatism and functionality. We have carried these ideas with us into the Christian life. Our churches and our evangelism have to "work."

Without negating the importance of theology, of structures and of the disciplines of the Christian life, we must admit there is something very playful about being a Christian and living the Christian life. The grace of God in Christ has placed us in the free space of being loved and forgiven. And the playful Spirit, who goes where it wills, is the renewing, beautifying and empowering breath of God. This Spirit brings a kaleidoscope of grace and charisms into our lives and ever draws us into the mystery of God, the joy of community and the blessedness of service. These freeing and empowering spaces and graces—and the very mystery of who God is as a community of three Persons—invite us to superfluidity of worship, adoration and praise.

Martin Luther King speaks of worship under its more functional dimension: "Worship at its best is a social experience with people of all levels of life coming together to realize their oneness and unity under God."[54] That too is a part of worship. But it is not the heart of worship.

Worship at its heart is an extravagant response of our life to God because of his extraordinary love and generosity toward us. Thus worship is both personal and communal. It involves adoration and service.

Worship is not a means to some end. Worship has God in view and the joy of being loved by this God and of loving him in return.

Reflection: "Through Jesus, therefore, let us continually offer to God a sacrifice of praise—the fruit of lips that confess his name. And do not forget to do good and to share with others, for with such sacrifices God is pleased" (Hebrews 13:15–16).

55

Work

Using Our Creativity for the World's Betterment

God is a worker. God created the heavens and the earth. We are made in God's image. And we too are creative and are called to be workers. But in our world, meaningful work is for the few. Mundane work is for the many. And no work is the increasing reality of our world. With this latter reality we are wounding the image of God in the human being.

Martin Luther King is adamant: "In our society it is murder, psychologically, to deprive a [person] of a job or an income."[55] There are many reasons this is so. And being helped by the welfare system is not the ultimate solution.

The most basic reason unemployment is not only unhelpful but destructive is that it goes against the very nature of who we are. This is not to suggest that we are *only* workers. Nor does it suggest that rest, Sabbath and retirement are not appropriate. But being a worker flows from the idea that God the Worker has created us and calls us to care for and shape the created order. Thus as human beings we are invited to participate in building family, neighborhood, church and institutions, and to participate in the care and formation of the human community.

But to be excluded from making our contribution, to have no role to play, and to make nothing is a deadening experience. Not to be able to use our energy, gifts and abilities—no matter whether they are great or small—leaves one without some of the central realities of what it means to be a human being.

King is right, but the sad thing is that our world has accepted that unemployment is the price we have to pay for contemporary capitalism. And the church has long fallen silent on this matter. So we create soup kitchens rather than jobs, and thus we add to people's psychological and sociological dislocation.

Reflection: "A man can do nothing better than to eat and drink and find satisfaction in his work. This too, I see, is from the hand of God" (Ecclesiastes 2:24).

56

The Complete Life

Integrating the Personal, Spiritual and Social

One of the sad realities of the Western approach to life is that we segment certain areas from others: the personal from the social, the spiritual from the political and the communal from the institutional. But, finally, we can't really live this way. Life is interconnected. And the biblical vision is that all of life is lived to the glory of God and for the well-being of the neighbor.

It is understandable that we find it difficult to hold all the elements of our lives together. It is far easier to prioritize certain things and ignore or neglect others. Thus some people prioritize work over family or activism over prayer. It is far more difficult to live in a series of concentric circles where attention is given to personal space, family, church, work and care for the neighbor.

But can such a life be lived? It can only be lived by embracing the biblical vision of life. Martin Luther King articulates this integrated vision in this way: "Love your neighbor as yourself. . . . That is the breadth of life. But . . . there is a first and even greater commandment, 'Love the Lord thy God with all thy heart and all thy soul and all thy mind.' This is the height of life."[56] The breadth of life comes out of the height of life. Out of the love of God and love for God comes love of neighbor. And this makes life complete.

Why is this both a wonderful and challenging way to live?

One answer is that it gives rightful attention to both the Creator and the creature. Another answer is that it brings spirituality and social concern together. And, finally, it connects my personal world with the reign of God and service to my neighbor.

All of this is particularly challenging because we so readily want to make ourselves the center, and so use God or the neighbor for our own ends. But for us to truly live, God must be at the center, and only by living in God's presence can we truly love ourselves and those within our sphere of contact.

Reflection: "Be imitators of God, therefore, as dearly loved children and live a life of love, just as Christ loved us and gave himself up for us as a fragrant offering and sacrifice to God" (Ephesians 5:1–2).

57

The Black Christ

A Christology Beyond Stereotype

Jesus was incarnated as a Jew. But he is also the Son of Man and the Son of God. He is both the human being and the Lord of history. As such, Jesus is for everyone and for every culture. He is thus for Asians, for Africans, for Hispanics and for those in the West.

Martin Luther King had to grapple with a great disconnect. For many, Jesus was seen as a white person, and Christianity was seen as a Western religion. Yet it was whites and the West that were oppressing King's people. While James Cone and others went on to formulate a theology of the black Christ, King is clear "that Jesus Christ was not a white man. [And] Christianity is not just a Western religion."[57]

For the first fourteen hundred years, Christianity was predominantly non-Western. And today, after a period of Western dominance, the majority of Christians live in the Two-Thirds World, while Christianity in the West continues to weaken.

In different times and cultures Jesus is portrayed as Chinese, Hispanic, or black. What does this mean? It does not mean that there is a denial that Jesus was the Son of Man, *the* human One. The One God who becomes flesh.

But as Christianity has become indigenized, each culture has celebrated the fact that Christ does not belong primarily to one group. He is Son of Man and Son of God for all. This then becomes the missional repetition of the Incarnation. Jesus is not only not a white man, but he is one who identifies himself with the poor and the oppressed. In this identification we can speak of the black Christ because Christ is for African-Americans.

Because Christ came to set captives free and open prison doors, and because he came to heal and renew, he is truly for all who need his grace, healing and freedom. No culture, no society can lay exclusive claim to Jesus Christ. Christ is the One who came to give his life for the world, and as such he belongs to all who embrace him.

Reflection: "Then Peter began to speak: 'I now realize how true it is that God does not show favoritism but accepts men from every nation who fear him and do what is right'" (Acts 10:34–35).

58

The Failure of Silence

The Deadening of the Prophetic Voice

The God of the Bible is the God who speaks. We who have come to faith in God are also invited to speak. We speak to God in prayer and we speak to the world in prophecy. These two forms of speaking are closely related. We cannot speak to God without also speaking to the world about God's forgiveness and healing. And we cannot speak to the world without praying for its transformation.

While the church is to be hidden seed in the form of the praying community, it is also to be scattered seed in the form of witness and prophecy. The church can never be a silent community of faith. This is not to suggest that the church should be involved in any and every kind of speaking. The word of the community of faith addressed to the world is the word of the good news that in Christ all are invited to new life. In proclaiming good news, the church must also identify what is bad news. It must address the false promises of our contemporary culture and identify the idolatries of our time.

But on both fronts it seems that the church has fallen silent. The church in the West is no longer that certain about the gospel, and it has become a culturally captive church. Thus it fails to speak on behalf of God and fails to speak on behalf of the oppressed in our world.

Martin Luther King had this to say: "We will have to repent in this generation not merely for the hateful words and actions of the bad people, but for the appalling silence of the good people."[58] While good people are not the only ones in the community of faith, the church should nevertheless raise its voice in good and bad times to proclaim the reign of God and to call for peace and justice in our world. Often the church has been silent. Self-preoccupied or uncertain about the issues—or lacking in courage—the church has not cried out on behalf of the needy, the poor, the marginalized and the oppressed.

The failure of prophecy may well be the failure of prayer. The failure to speak to the world may well be the failure to be close to the heart of God.

Reflection: "Return, faithless people; I will cure you of backsliding" (Jeremiah 3:22).

59

The Ultimate Cost

The Final Self-Giving in the Service of Justice

There are vocations in both the church and the world that have to do with strengthening what already is. These are important contributions. There are also vocations that challenge what is and call for transformation. While the one is more a priestly task, the latter is more a prophetic task. And prophets are most likely to be vilified or killed.

After the assassination of John F. Kennedy, Martin Luther King began to be increasingly aware of the fact that he too could one day be killed. In fact, he came to see that this was not simply implicit in the madness of the world, but was embedded in the vocation of the prophet. King noted, "Before the victory of justice is a reality, some may even face physical death."[59] Sadly, this became a reality for King.

And what about us who have never been called onto the national stage, but nevertheless seek to be servants of the reign of God? The very nature of being called to be a Christian is to embrace various deaths.

The first form of death is to abandon our own willful ways and to begin to live in Christ's kingdom of reconciliation and peace under Christ's lordship and direction. The commitment to baptism symbolizes and affirms this initial death. We have died to our old ways to embrace Christ's new way for us.

But there are also other forms of death. One is to enter into various expressions of asceticism. Here we voluntarily and for the sake of Christ say no to some of the good things of life. We do this not because we think these good things are bad, but because we want to make space for worship, prayer and service.

The other form of death is where we lay down our life for the service of Christ. And whether we are serving Christ in the home or in the public arena, in the pulpit or in politics, it matters not. Whether this service is on the foreign mission field or in the workplace, it matters not, as long as it is Christ we are serving.

Reflection: "This is how we know what love is: Jesus Christ laid down his life for us. And we ought to lay down our lives for our brothers" (1 John 3:16).

60

Following the Spirit

Seeing the God Who Is Ahead of Us

From the biblical story, it is clear that God has been and continues to be involved in our world. However, the signs of his presence are not always immediately obvious. And sometimes God is at work in unexpected places. Therefore, we need the eyes of faith and the gift of discernment.

Martin Luther King rightly believed that the Spirit of God was at work, not only in the community of faith, but also in the world. And so he counseled that we must "keep our ears open to the spirit."[60]

To identify the work of the Spirit in the community of faith is not so difficult. When people grow in love and demonstrate the fruit of the Spirit, we can say that the Spirit is graciously present. When people are empowered by the charisms of the Spirit, we can rejoice that the Spirit is at work. When people come to faith in Christ, we can attribute this to the work of the Spirit. And when the community of faith reaches out to neighbors and colleagues to bring help, hope and love, we can see that they are moved by the Spirit.

Discerning the work of the Spirit in the world is much more difficult. One way we can think about this is to recognize that whenever and wherever good occurs and people are made more whole, there the Spirit is at work. Or more specifically, wherever through good means the world is made more just, more peaceful, and more generous-hearted, there too the Spirit is moving, transforming and empowering.

However, whether in the world or in the church, we must be careful not to identify all that happens with the work of the Holy Spirit. Our work and the Spirit's are not synonymous. In fact, there are many times when the Spirit needs to subvert our work. This happens particularly when our work is self-serving, and is not for the greater good.

A particular challenge for most of us is that we think God's Spirit works only in particular ways. But so often the Spirit works unexpectedly and uses the most unlikely people.

Reflection: "Where can I go from your Spirit? Where can I flee from your presence? If I go up to the heavens, you are there; if I make my bed in the depths, you are there" (Psalm 139:7–8).

61

Courage

THE ABILITY TO PRESS ON AGAINST THE ODDS

The most celebrated and sought-after of all Christian virtues are faith, hope and love. And love is regarded as the cardinal virtue. But each of these virtues calls for an ancillary grace: courage.

Ours is a complex and refractory world. It is a world marked by beauty and goodness. It is also marred by selfishness, violence and idolatry. Those who seek to do good in our world have no simple and smooth path in front of them. It is not as if the world cries out a warm welcome: Come and bless us with your good and your God!

So often, the opposite seems to be the case. The good is resisted, particularly when the good is not about reinforcing the status quo or benefiting those who already have much. When the good is subversive and transformative—seeking to bless the poor and challenging those in power—then the good is often stonewalled.

Persistence in praying and working for God's good to come to fuller expression in our communities, neighborhoods and institutions calls for fortitude, perseverance and courage. Martin Luther King knew something about this in his efforts to bring about racial integration, to end poverty, and to resist war-mongering. He wrote, "Courage faces fear and thereby masters it. Cowardice represses fear and is thereby mastered by it."[61]

So we are called to live in hope that evil need not hold sway. We live in faith that God is working and that things can change. We live in love, seeking God's goodness and the conversion of oppressors. But we also need the gift of courage to face resistance and opposition.

No major moral victory is ever won easily. Evil needs to be exposed and deposed. And goodness has to overcome evil. This requires courage, which commits us to following God's peaceable Spirit in the face of violence. We follow God's transformative Spirit in the face of resistance, and God's gracious Spirit in the face of all bitterness and hatred.

There are times when we lack not knowledge or love, but courage in committing ourselves to doing what we must.

Reflection: "Be strong and courageous, because you will lead these people to inherit the land" (Joshua 1:6).

62

The Call

Responding to God or to the Need?

Discerning God's call or hearing the voice of God or knowing the will of God has always been a difficult process. How can we be sure that it's God who is calling us? What if we are responding to need's call or are reacting out of our own issues, needs, or dysfunctions?

Not only are societies complex, but we too are complex and multifaceted creatures. We both know ourselves and are a mystery to ourselves. And the reasons we do things, respond in certain ways, and take on particular causes are both known to us and lie in the darkness of the complex persons that we are.

So what about the voice and the will of God then? How do we know that God is calling us to certain tasks? How did Martin Luther King know that he was being called to become a social reformer? King felt the call to take on a leadership role in the civil rights movement through a complexity of factors. But rather than receiving the call through some mystical experience, King responded to the opportunities and needs in front of him.

King likened his call to that of the apostle Paul's: "Like Paul, I must constantly respond to the Macedonian call."[62] But this was no mere visionary experience. King understood the times in which he lived. He saw the liberation of the peoples of the Third World, throwing off the shackles of colonialism. He also understood the crushing humiliation of his own people as second-rate citizens in the land of the free and the brave. And the events that led to the Montgomery bus boycott threw King into a position of leadership.

Thus being called by God is always a multi-layered affair. Our prior preparation and gifting, the particular circumstances, the need and challenges, and the tugs of the Holy Spirit all combine to give us a sense of God's particular calling. While we may be called by a direct visionary experience, God can work in many ways to bring us to the task he has chosen for us.

Reflection: "The LORD said, 'I have indeed seen the misery of my people in Egypt. . . . So I have come down to rescue them. . . . So now, go. I am sending you to Pharaoh to bring my people the Israelites out of Egypt'" (Exodus 3:7, 8, 10).

63

Interiority

THE STRENGTH OF THE INNER LIFE

In asking the question, "What makes a person, a community, or a nation strong?" we may be tempted to look first at the external resources at one's command. But in the final analysis this is not where true strength and greatness lie. It lies instead in the hope, faith, love and courage of the heart.

While we are all readily impressed with the external trappings of greatness, power and strength, we must not be fooled into thinking that this is where real strength lies. True strength lies within. It is a matter of the heart. Thus the heart matters.

The strength of the Christian life does not lie in one's position and power. It lies in the empowerment that comes from within. It has to do with being shaped, sustained, beautified and gifted by the Spirit.

The circumstances may be difficult, the times hard and the social landscape bleak, but these realities need not define and shape us. Through the blessing of hope crafted by the Spirit in our inner being, it is possible to live *against* unfavorable circumstances rather than be overwhelmed by them.

Martin Luther King assures us that God "gives us the interior resources to bear the burdens and tribulations of life."[63] These inner resources have nothing to do with living in denial or in an unrealistic utopianism. Neither a head-in-the-sand attitude nor daydreaming for a new tomorrow will really empower us. Instead, it is the belief that God is with us in the midst of our struggles that is truly life-giving.

The interior resources that will sustain us in difficult times are not resignation and fatalism, but hope in the God of the Exodus, who hears the cry of his people and draws near to comfort, sustain, empower and liberate. These resources are not of our own making. They are the gifts of God for the people of God. They are the charisms of grace. This is the mothering presence of the Holy Spirit birthing within us the gifts of faith and hope.

Inner strength in difficult times is a greater blessing than outward blessing in times of ease. The former will sculpt us more fully into the image of God.

Reflection: "Therefore we do not lose heart. Though outwardly we are wasting away, yet inwardly we are being renewed day by day" (2 Corinthians 4:16).

64

Transformation

A Changed Self, a Changed Society

Unfortunately, the various branches of the Christian community are not always on the same page. And where this is most evident is regarding the mission of the church. Some believe the primary calling of the church is to change people through the work of evangelism. Others believe that the church is called to change social structures.

The calling and mission of the church can never be reduced to a single and particular task. Nor should it be cast in either/or categories. Because the church is called to be a servant, sign and sacrament of the reign of God, its mission must be understood in comprehensive terms. It is bringing the whole gospel to the world in both word and deed. This flows out of the vision that God's redemptive purposes include persons, families and communities. In fact, all of life, including the created order, will find its fulfillment in Christ.

Therefore Martin Luther King is right regarding the all-embracing nature of God's transformative activity. He notes, "All radicals understand the need for action—direct self-transformation and structure-transforming action."[64] Transformation can never remain at the level of ideas. Transformation must lead to action that changes things.

While we may often think that the place to start is to change others, this is not the case. Change must start with us. We must turn to Christ. We must be converted. We must be more fully converted! We must not only be peacemakers, we must be peaceful. We must not only be reconcilers, we must ourselves be reconciled.

Being on the way of our own radical transformation, we are called to cooperate with God in his transformational activity in our world. And this involves seeing God's reign come to fruition in the hearts of individuals, but also in our communities and institutions.

But it is one thing to share the good news of Christ with an individual. It is quite another to see social structures change to reflect more fully God's kingdom. This calls for careful and thoughtful work in seeing God's shalom and justice more fully embedded in our social world.

Reflection: "Seek justice, encourage the oppressed. Defend the cause of the fatherless, plead the case of the widow" (Isaiah 1:17).

65

A Reluctant Church

The Church in Flight from the World

Throughout its over two-thousand-year journey, the church has taken different postures in its relation to the world. At one extreme it has sought politically to control the world. At the other end of the spectrum it has adopted a world-denying and world-escaping form of Christianity. In between lie more biblical options.

Martin Luther King lived the vision that Christians should not turn their backs to the world, but should actively engage the world so that the light of God's kingdom becomes more fully realized in our beautiful but broken world. He believed that Christians should be in the forefront in working for change.

Not all share this vision. And historically, the community of faith has not always played that role in our world. King sadly notes, "All too often the religious community has been a tail light instead of a head light."[65]

There are many reasons why it is not helpful for the church to take this posture, but the most basic is that it flies in the face of the biblical vision regarding the role of the people of God in the world. At the heart of the biblical story is a vision of a God who loves the world and seeks its healing and transformation. This story recognizes the forces of evil and darkness in our world and notes that these are not just in some people and communities, but in all people. Therefore all need to be transformed by God's love and grace, and all need to be made whole.

From the place of being touched by the wideness of God's mercy and shaped by the renewing Spirit, people then live with the desire to see others blessed and transformed—not only solitary individuals, but the whole social order. Christians are called to be in the forefront of peacemaking, reconciliation and healing. They are called to be prophets who cry out for justice. They are to be the workers who seek to bring God's good to our world.

King's pioneering work against racism, poverty and war can be an example for all of us. And God may well call others to pioneer not only in the work of social justice, but also in all the other fields of human endeavor.

Reflection: "And he said to me, 'Son of man, listen carefully and take to heart all the words I speak to you. Go now to your countrymen in exile and speak to them'" (Ezekiel 3:10–11).

66

The Love of God

Living the Goodness of God in a Refractory World

For many in our contemporary world the goodness and love of God is a difficult notion. God is seen as distant and arbitrary, and by some as angry and vindictive. While this perspective may be excusable because people have suffered abuse at the hands of the church, the angry God is not the central motif of the biblical story.

There are times when we question the love of God. When harm comes to those we love, we wonder not only why this had to happen, but also why God did not stop it. If God is all-powerful, as we confess, then surely God had the power to prevent this tragedy. But tragedy continues. Disasters occur. And death is a reality.

The biblical story does not invite us to contemplate the vindictive God or the powerless God, but calls us to reflect on the strange connection between God and humanity. God rescues his people in the Exodus event, but he also sends them into Babylonian captivity. God heals, but suffering is also part of the Christian's journey. Scripture's invitation, therefore, is to trust the God who speaks and is silent, the God who protects us from harm and the God who wounds us, the God who gives so generously, but who also invites us into desert places.

Martin Luther King once made this observation: "It is quite easy for me to think of a God of love mainly because I grew up in a family where love was central and where loving relationships were ever present."[66] He is right. One's family context is important for one's religious experience.

But in a loveless world, one can still come to see God as loving, because that is how God has disclosed himself in Scripture. The God of the Bible enters our world of pain and suffering and in the world to come will fully eradicate these from our lives. In the meantime, we experience grace for the difficult journey, hope in the face of doubt, sustenance in the barren places, and the comfort of God's Spirit in the places of questioning and ambiguity.

Reflection: "The LORD is slow to anger, abounding in love and forgiving sin and rebellion" (Numbers 14:18).

67

Deceitful Concessions

CRUMBS FROM THE RICH PERSON'S TABLE

While generosity and justice can come from those in power, this is seldom the case. Justice is more commonly the demand of the poor and oppressed than the gift of the powerful, although those in power may give concessions that ultimately change little.

Martin Luther King was quick to realize that when enough pressure was applied, those in power were willing to make concessions. But so often these concessions are deceitful. They give the appearance of generosity. But at the end of the day nothing much changes. Hence King's pertinent comment, "There is a critical distinction . . . between a modest start and tokenism."[67]

Pharaoh was willing to make concessions to the demands of Moses. But finally, these were deceitful. Those who press for change on behalf of the poor and oppressed do, eventually, get a hearing. And promises for help and change are eventually made. But so often little changes. These promises are like the new growth that springs up in shallow soil. And soon the blistering sun of disappointment withers everything away.

Working for change in the major structures of our society is no fly-by-night experience. Major changes usually do not come quickly or easily. And the tactic of delay can wear one down. Thus perseverance is called for. But more fundamentally, those working for change must be clear about their end goals lest they settle for the compromises that are so readily offered.

The biblical vision does not have the majority in view when it expresses its vision of justice. It has *the least* in view. When love, generosity and justice are extended to the "little ones" in a society, then the kingdom of God is breaking in. True change has not taken place when the change agents are blessed, but when the least are blessed.

Reflection: "Moses answered, 'We will go with our young and old, with our sons and daughters, and with our flocks and herds, because we are to celebrate a festival to the LORD.' Pharaoh said, '. . . No! Have only the men go; and worship the LORD'" (Exodus 10:9–11).

68

Success

The Biblical Vision of Self-Giving

Success in the West is usually understood as being popular, powerful and having an abundance of resources. The biblical story does not speak of success but of obedience and doing the will of God. In the Christian framework, success is recast into conformity to Christ and loving service to neighbor.

There are probably as many definitions of success as there are cultures to define it. And success has been understood differently in different historical periods. For us, in the contemporary West, a successful person is someone who has made an outstanding achievement in his or her profession, whether that is the arts, commerce, politics, or any other field of human endeavor. And this person has been publicly recognized as such and has been rewarded for it. This idea of success has to do with public valuation. It may have nothing to do with a person's private life.

Martin Luther King looks at success very differently: "We are prone to judge success by the index of our salaries . . . rather than by the quality of our service and relationship to humanity."[68] Here success does not have in view what you have become or what you have achieved or accumulated. Success in this paradigm looks at what you have given away and how you have enriched others.

This approximates the biblical vision. Here the idea is not a focus on *your* success, but on *another's* well-being. In Scripture the vision is self-giving not to enhance the self, but self-giving in the service of others, particularly those who cannot give in return.

King is right in saying that life is not simply all about us. It is about the beloved community, humanity wrapped up in mutual care, encouragement and support. What we have given away in love and service defines us much more than what we have. And the great surprise in the blessing of others is that we ourselves are enriched.

Reflection: "For even the Son of Man did not come to be served, but to serve, and to give his life as a ransom for many" (Mark 10:45).

69

Conflicted

Facing the Demons Within

We long for peace not only in our world, but also within our own being. That we are inwardly torn is a fact of our existence. We were created for love and goodness, but so much less than that is the fruit of our lives. So while we continue to strive to fulfill our higher aspirations, much of what we do is banal and at times downright sinful.

Martin Luther King has articulated the conflictual nature of human existence well. He observes, "There is something of a civil war going on within all our lives. . . . Within the best of us there is some evil, and within the worst of us there is some good."[69]

Sometimes the impression is given that coming to faith in Christ through the Holy Spirit will bring an end to this inner conflict. It is suggested that we will be at peace with God and all will be well. Not only is this not the case, but the opposite is in fact true. Inner conflict will increase when one comes to faith in Christ and seeks to live a life of discipleship. The more one grows in Christ and the more Christ's life is formed in us by the Holy Spirit, the more conflict will increase. And it does so in two ways. First, growth in holiness deepens our sense of our own sinfulness. Second, in the obedient following of Jesus we are frequently not faced with making choices between good and evil, but between good and greater good. And this is difficult to discern and to live.

All of this is simply to say that being a Christian involves embracing the conflict within. The call to the fuller embrace of the kingdom of God invites challenge, conversion and transformation. Growth in the desire to live for God's glory and for God's kingdom purposes will constantly invite us to be open to change and to lay aside our own direction and priorities.

Thus, though embraced by the forgiving and renewing love of Christ, the Christian is still a sinner in need of God's grace. And hence one's prayer will always be: Lord, do a deeper renewing work in me.

Reflection: "Here is a trustworthy saying that deserves full acceptance: Christ Jesus came into the world to save sinners—of whom I am the worst. But for that very reason I was shown mercy" (1 Timothy 1:15–16).

70

Between Promise and Fulfillment

The Long Journey of Faith and Hope

When we are caught up in the forward movement of history, when significant change is taking place, we become hopeful that almost anything is possible. But change is always provisional and anticipatory. We will always be in the midst of change and in the way of change. Thus change is always more hope than fulfillment.

Martin Luther King was often frustrated by the lack of progress in hoped-for change. And he rightly points out that "the gap between promise and fulfillment is distressingly wide."[70] But not only is there a gap between other people's promises and our hoped-for expectations—such a gap also lies within ourselves. We also cannot deliver all that we would like to bring to the change process. And to the work of change we also bring our own weaknesses and failures. Thus we don't live up to our own promises. This is a sobering assessment. It also is a potentially liberating one.

We work for change. We pray much. We do what we can. We join with others in the work. But our very best will always be the few loaves and fishes that a boy brought to Jesus. Ours is but a small offering, and God will have to give the increase. This is no resignation to settle for something less. It is a call to recognize the limitations within which we do our faithful and committed work.

Only God himself can bridge the gap between promise and fulfillment. In Christ, God is both the promise and the fulfillment of the inbreaking reign of God and its consummation in the age to come. Through the prophetic charisms of the Spirit, we can begin the good work. But we can't complete it. Only God can do that. And in that hope we serve and pray.

Reflection: "He [Jesus] could not do any miracles there, except lay his hands on a few sick people and heal them. And he was amazed at their lack of faith" (Mark 6:5–6).

71

Prophet-Priest

Living the Lordship of Christ

In classical Protestant theology we speak of the three "offices" of Christ: prophet, priest and king. The church as the body of Christ is called to participate in these functions of Christ. We are called to kingly, prophetic and priestly service in the world.

When it has been a healthy community of faith, the church has always understood itself as existing for God, for one another and for service to the world. In its service to the world, the church has understood this in comprehensive terms. All of life is to be impacted by God's saving grace and by the values of the kingdom of God.

The church as sign, sacrament and servant of the kingdom is to express Christ's kingly, prophetic and priestly ministries in the world. The kingly calls all to a life of obedience. The prophetic invites all into the service of justice and transformation. And the priestly invites all into prayer and the healing dimensions of the gospel. In his work of social transformation, Martin Luther King wanted to keep this vision of the church's role in the forefront of his thinking and praxis. He reminds us, "I happen to be a minister of the gospel . . . and in that capacity I have not merely a priestly function but [also] a prophetic function."[71]

People seem to be most happy when the church exercises only its priestly function. Worship, prayer, encouragement, healing—these are all important roles the church can play. The church's prophetic function is less readily understood and appreciated. A frequent sentiment is: Should not the church focus on its spiritual responsibilities and leave other matters to the politicians?

But this idea must be rejected. The church is not only concerned about a person's soul, but also about the total person. The church is to bring God's good news to individuals, but also to the whole society. And the church has a task in calling the powerful of this world to the work of justice. Both God's healing presence and God's passion for the poor and needy are to be embodied in the church and proclaimed to the world.

Reflection: "I will search for the lost and bring back the strays . . . but the sleek and the strong I will destroy. I will shepherd the flock with justice" (Ezekiel 34:16).

72

The Oppressive Power of Hate

Walking the Long Road of Love

To walk the long road of love within a family or community of care and respect is not all that difficult. But to walk that road in relation to one's enemies is. Love in the face of hatred is not a mere human capacity but an impartation of grace.

While it is conceivable that a person may be essentially a hateful person, hate is usually not intrinsic but is a reaction. Hate is a temptation that comes our way. It is a temptation we are called to resist, but one to which we sometimes or frequently surrender.

Hate is the most immediate temptation when one has been unjustly wronged. When a whole people has been wronged, not just on a particular occasion but for multiple decades, temptation's power seems almost irresistible. And so hate spirals into ever greater and more defuse hatred. The hated and despised then turn and hate the perpetrators.

Martin Luther King clearly understood that hatred would not empower his people. He was sure the opposite was the case, noting, "Hate scars the soul and distorts the personality."[72] And so King called for another way: the way of nonviolent protest and resistance based on love rather than on hatred toward those in power.

Yes, hatred is finally a destructive force. And its greatest destruction is not what people may do by way of retaliation. Hatred is a cancer in the soul of the oppressed and marginalized. Its power shapes who we are and defines what we do. It may empower for the moment, but it demoralizes for a lifetime. It may produce a momentary sweet revenge, but it yields a life of bitterness.

Hatred is the way of the anti-reign. It is not the way of God's kingdom. The seeming weakness of forgiveness and love is finally more powerful than the apparent strength of hatred and retaliation.

Reflection: "Love does no harm to its neighbor. Therefore love is the fulfillment of the law" (Romans 13:10).

73

Challenge for the Church

The Call to Be God's Radical Community

The church is one of the most enduring institutions of our world. It has existed for over two thousand years. And throughout that long journey of history, the church has been both a powerful institution and a despised minority. But whether strong or weak, it first and foremost has been called to be a faithful witness to the gospel of God's good news in Christ.

While the church in the Third World continues to grow with unabated pace, the church in the West continues to lose ground. Western Christianity is in deep trouble theologically and morally.

In the days of the struggle for civil rights for African-Americans, Martin Luther King was himself struggling with the role of the church. He felt that the church was too silent on matters of justice and that it was too much committed to the status quo. So he constantly appealed to the church to not be afraid and to play its part.

Within this framework, King threw out his prophetic challenge: "If today's church does not recapture the sacrificial spirit of the early church, it will lose its authenticity, forfeit the loyalty of millions and be dismissed as an irrelevant social club."[73] Many decades later we can see the relevance of these words. Much of what King said then has come true.

What is of note in King's challenge to the church is the call to return to the spirit of early Christianity. This is a restitutionist call. It's a call to recover the vision and ethos of the gospel. This is a call we all the more urgently need to hear today.

The early Christians were sure that Jesus had risen from the dead and that he was the Savior of the world. They were sure that the risen Christ had poured out the Holy Spirit upon them. They were sure that living in the joy of the faith they could live a life of obedience, suffering and service. Forming communities of faith and hospitality, the early Christians extended a welcome to all, including the poor and needy, to sit at the banquet table of God's love.

In recapturing the power of the risen Christ through the Spirit, we too can become communities of love, faith and hope that challenge the dominant values of secular culture.

Reflection: "After they prayed . . . they were all filled with the Holy Spirit and spoke the word of God boldly" (Acts 4:31).

74

Riches

Their Alluring Power

The Western world sees itself as dominant, powerful and self-sufficient. And the Western values of materialism, individualism, consumerism and militarism are dominant realities. The church in the West has become infected by these values and is losing its spiritual power.

Martin Luther King's observation is pertinent and deeply troubling: "The richer we have become materially, the poorer we have become morally and spiritually."[74] As a broad generalization of the Western church, this appears to be the case. So are there any answers to this sad state of affairs?

The first observation I wish to make is that I know some people who are very rich but who are deeply spiritually committed. Second, I know of well-to-do churches that are spiritually alive, evangelistically active and committed to serving the poor. What these two observations suggest is that while King's observation is broadly correct, it need not be this way.

And this is the point I wish to press. Just as poverty is not the automatic gateway to spirituality, so material well-being is not the automatic door to spiritual indifference. This, of course, is not to suggest that riches do not pose a problem. Having much can make us proud, self-sufficient and uncaring. Riches can pervert our life with God through the Spirit. But it need not be so! We can love God more than our material possessions. We can live the blessed state of generosity. We can have much and see God as the center of our lives as the gracious giver of all good things.

It is possible to be rich and to have a vision for the kingdom and to serve the poor. I know such people. And they are saints indeed, having resisted the alluring power of riches by making Christ Lord of their lives. But what a challenge for the church in the West, with all its material blessings, to seek the riches of God's kingdom!

Reflection: "But Zacchaeus stood up and said to the Lord, 'Look, Lord! Here and now I give half of my possessions to the poor, and if I have cheated anybody out of anything, I will pay back four times the amount'" (Luke 19:8).

75

Significance

Living Life's True Meaning

We humans are meaning-making creatures. We seek to make meaning of our world and of our own lives. And as such, we ask the questions: What is truly worthwhile and purposeful? What is important and significant? While many differing answers have been suggested, the Christian vision links our significance to being loved by God.

No one wants to be a nobody. As human beings, we have a sense that life should be meaningful and purposeful. It should have significance. And this becomes the garb that embodies our identity. In our contemporary world, our significance very quickly becomes confused with our functionality and performance. It is because I achieve well and do much that I am significant.

This idea is also communicated or subtly implied in the community of faith. My worth has to do with my spiritual performance. It is possible that Martin Luther King also leans too much in that direction. He writes that a person "has cosmic significance if he [or she] is serving humanity and doing the will of God."[75]

Now, this is true. What we do in serving God in our ministry to the world can have eternal significance. To bring a person to faith in Christ, to serve the cause of justice, to bring healing and reconciliation are all realities for this life and the life to come.

But my ultimate significance does not lie in what I do, produce and achieve. It lies delightfully and iconoclastically elsewhere. It lies in the miracle of being loved by the cosmic Lover.

My significance is more truly defined by the *imago Dei,* by Christ's death on my behalf, by the gift of the Spirit, and by the embrace of God the Father. The miracle of who I am is that God loves me. From eternity he loved me, and in covenant faithfulness he continues to love and hold me, even though my response to this love is woefully weak. From this place of love and embrace I can bless others and do things that are important in the kingdom of God.

Reflection: "When Israel was a child, I loved him, and out of Egypt I called my son" (Hosea 11:1).

76

In the Middle

Standing at the Convergence of Two Streams

Those who articulate a new vision for the human community frequently find themselves betwixt and between. For the traditionalists, one is seen as too radical. For the radicals, one is seen as not radical enough. Caught in the middle, the role of mediation becomes a critical calling. This task is often a cross-bearing effort.

Martin Luther King made it clear that within the African-American community he was not everyone's hero. He also pointed out that the community was divided: "I stand in the middle of two opposing forces in the [African-American] community. One is a force of complacency. . . . The other is one of bitterness and hatred."[76]

He was referring to those who could not or would not see the purpose of change and those who believed that much more radical change strategies should be adopted rather than King's nonviolent resistance. Anyone who has worked for communal and social change knows what King is talking about. Change is always carried forward by creative visionaries, but is resisted by fearful conservatives and hotheaded radicals who want more than what is possible.

This being in the middle of two forces is also true for the Christian life. The Christian stands where two forces meet: the will of God and the will of the world. Put more theologically, the Christian experiences the "nowness" of the kingdom of God breaking into life, community and world, but the Christian also experiences the anti-reign and the "not yet" realities of the kingdom. Thus the Christian lives in the middle. He or she also lives in the middle of what God has already done in Christ in the past and what God will yet do in the eschatological future.

Christians live between the times. They are in the middle. They are called forward into the vision of the reign of God. They are tempted backward into Satan's anti-reign. All of this is a difficult way to live. In fact, this is the way of the Cross. It is living the will of God against the world, which we nevertheless love and care for. No one can live this way without the comforting and sustaining presence of God's Spirit.

Reflection: "Today I have made you a fortified city, an iron pillar and a bronze wall to stand against the whole land" (Jeremiah 1:18).

77

Cross-Bearing

Living the Cruciform Life

It is a serious misconception that the Christian life is only one of blessing and well-being. This has in view only what we receive. But the Christian life also has to do with what we become through God's transformative activity. And it has to do with what we are called to give. Thus, more accurately, the Christian life is one of receiving and giving, blessing and suffering, and experiencing the resurrection life of God as well as the Cross.

Martin Luther King did not advocate a bless-me gospel of cheap grace. His vision of being a Christian was radically different. This vision is clearly articulated in one of his sermons, in which he says, "To be a Christian, one must take up [one's] cross with all of its difficulties . . . and carry it until that very cross leaves its marks upon us and redeems us to that more excellent way which comes only through suffering."[77]

While it is most understandable that we seek to do all we can to avoid suffering and cross-bearing, we finally cannot, for these are laid on us by God's good hand. Cross-bearing and the suffering that accompanies it is not the work of the Enemy. It is the work of the heavenly Friend, who seeks our deeper and fuller transformation.

The secret of the Christian life is not only to receive the blessings that come from Christ's death on our behalf. It is also to have the death and resurrection of Christ repeated in our lives. Christ died on our behalf. That is true. But we are also called to die on his behalf. In other words, we are to lay down our own ways in order to serve him alone. Christ rose to bring new life to all. That is true. But the resurrection life of Christ must also be repeated in us so that we can bring new life to others.

Cross-bearing is God's call to us all. Its seeming heavy weight also has a lightness, for cross-bearing is not a curse. It is the strange blessing in the hand of God to conform us more fully to the image of his Son.

Reflection: "May I never boast except in the cross of our Lord Jesus Christ, through which the world has been crucified to me, and I to the world" (Galatians 6:14).

78

Vulnerability

Opening to Others Our Weakness and Struggles

Some Christians have the idea that they should appear strong before others and weak before God. They believe living this way is a testimony to God's provision and grace. But so much in the biblical story points us in another direction. It is also in weakness that we honor the goodness of God.

I am quite sure that Martin Luther King, as the key civil rights leader, lived under the pressure of always having to appear as being strong and decisive. So much depended on him and so many people looked to him for inspiration and leadership. But King was not always strong. And he had demons to fight within. Like all of us, he had his internal issues and struggles as well as the outside opposition that constantly confronted him.

In a moment of transparent vulnerability, King cried out, "Lord, I'm down here trying to do what's right. . . . But Lord, I'm faltering, I'm losing my courage. And I can't let the people see me like this. . . . But I've come to the point where I can't face it alone."[78]

All those in positions of leadership may come to a similar point, particularly when working for difficult social change. So where does one turn? Well, one can't turn to just anyone. One could turn to one's pastor or a soul friend or a spiritual director. With such a companion we don't major on our strengths and achievements. We major on the movement of what is happening within. We major on our struggles of faith and courage. We major on our shadow side. We face our fears.

While this ministry of spiritual companionship has long been part of sacramental churches, Protestants and evangelicals are finally catching up. They too are seeing the importance of soul care. And they are beginning to realize that everything cannot be transacted simply between God and me.

There are times when we need to confess our sins to God, but in the presence of a soul friend. There are times where we need to open our struggles to God in the presence of another, a companion on the way.

Reflection: "Therefore confess your sins to each other and pray for each other so that you may be healed" (James 5:16).

79

Insecurities

Facing Our Inner Fears

It matters little what status we hold in life, what we have achieved, how rich we are and how popular we may be. These things never eradicate our more fundamental insecurities. We all have these insecurities, whether we acknowledge them or not. But it is far better to face them than to have them play tricks on us along life's pathway.

There are some Christians who hold the amazing idea that coming to faith in Christ is so radical and powerful that all the problems of our past are swept away at conversion. While we must in no way de-emphasize the powerful grace of Christ at conversion, this position collapses justification by faith into sanctification. Moreover, it makes our transformation a point in time rather than a process.

I believe that conversion calls us into a *journey* of faith where we grow in Christ and in Christlikeness. And in that journey we face not only the challenges and temptations of the future, but also the disappointments and woundedness of the past.

Martin Luther King hints at one of the issues we will need to continue to face: our insecurities. It matters little how far we have already come in life and how successful we may presently be. Our insecurities are ever with us, sculpted by the reality of our own sinfulness and through the brokenness, rejection and wounding we have experienced through the words and deeds of others.

King makes this more specific: "We are afraid of the superiority of other people, of failure and of the scorn or disapproval of those whose opinions we most value."[79] Our insecurities can take many other forms, but eventually they disempower us and may even immobilize us.

So what do we do? Most basically, instead of hiding our insecurities, we should face them and bring them into the open. Inviting the presence of the Spirit into our insecurities may not bring instant healing, but it will save us from the disabling pain of leaving things hidden.

Reflection: "I am feeble and utterly crushed; I groan in anguish of heart. All my longings lie open before you, O Lord; my sighing is not hidden from you" (Psalm 38:8–9).

80

The Depth of Love

Living Love's Transformational Power

Love is, at its most foundational level, a great gift, a deep mystery and a transformative power. That love has to be received in order for it to be given is to say the obvious. But a love that continues to spill out even toward one's enemies is a love that has been birthed in the womb of God.

There are many ways in which women and men exercise power within our world. They usually do so by virtue of the position they hold and the influence they exercise because of that position. Thus while a janitor and a president both have power, the latter's power is far greater because of that person's position.

But while we speak of positional and institutional power, we may also speak of moral power. This is power exercised by virtue of one's visionary ideas and one's character. Jesus was a mere tradesman. But the power of his vision of the kingdom of God and the power of his very person have greatly impacted our world. Thus it is also possible to speak of the power of love. This love is not self-seeking, but self-giving. There is power in such a love because it may totally transform the object of this love.

King understood this, as he explained, "*Agape* is understanding, creative, redemptive goodwill for all. . . . It is the love of God operating in the human heart. It is an over-flowing love that seeks nothing in return. . . . Love is a willingness to go the second mile in order to restore the broken community. Yes, love is even a willingness to die on a cross in order that others may live."[80]

The power of servant love and suffering love is the power not to persuade and certainly not to control. Rather, it is the power to disarm. It's a power that catches one by surprise. This is nutritive power—one that enriches, heals and renews. The power of this love builds up. It is restorative. It draws people together. It builds community. And it deepens our humanity.

This love is God's gift which we need to grow into and generously give away.

Reflection: "Love does not delight in evil but rejoices with the truth. It always protects, always trusts, always hopes, always perseveres" (1 Corinthians 13:6–7).

81

The Beginnings of Freedom

Beginning to Live the Unthinkable

Throughout history, men and women of goodwill and good intent have declared that a certain way is the way it is, and any other way is unthinkable and impossible. But there are others who have questioned this because they have seen another and a better way. Change, therefore, does not begin with action but with an alternate vision.

Social movements of freedom never begin in the place of freedom. They begin in the place of oppression. The vision of freedom for the Hebrew slaves in Egypt did not begin once they were across the Red Sea and finally into the Promised Land. The vision of freedom came in the midst of their hard and oppressive labor and pain.

Martin Luther King points out that "as long as the mind is enslaved the body can never be free."[81] Freedom has its genesis not in the light of one's experience of freedom but in the darkest night of one's oppression.

As long as people accept and submit to circumstances that already exist, nothing will change. But when a new vision is born deep within one's heart and soul that things can change, that things can and should be different, then a power is unleashed that no oppressor can subdue.

The blessing of a new vision of what can be—what ought to be—when born out of a biblical vision of the righteousness and justice of God, is a vision that like a candle can burn ever so brightly in even the darkest night. This vision birthed in hope and faith and inspired by the breath of God, the Holy Spirit, is a vision that makes the impossible possible.

This vision is usually carried by a significant leader, but for the vision to become a reality all the people must carry both the hope and the pain of bringing it to fulfillment.

Reflection: "Therefore, say to the Israelites: 'I am the LORD, and I will bring you out from under the yoke of the Egyptians. I will free you from being slaves to them, and I will redeem you'" (Exodus 6:6).

82

Unity and Diversity

Living the Kaleidoscope of God's Creativity

Anyone who looks at the natural world, unlike the world of urbanization, cannot but be struck by nature's amazing diversity. This bounteousness is also reflected in the world of human diversity and culture. This diversity should also be reflected in the church and in all the projects of faith.

In social change movements, in parachurch organizations and in the church itself there are those who argue for simplistic solutions and are governed by a monochrome approach to life. But single answers to complex problems do not work. Multiple strategies need to be employed to bring about change and transformation. Martin Luther King understood this well. He wrote, "Unity has never meant uniformity."[82] Those who argue for a narrow unity and singular solutions to complex problems are people who are insistent about control. And this can lead to intolerance of others.

While the Bible is blatantly clear that Yahweh alone is God and that Christ is the only way, truth and life, the Scriptures nevertheless sparkle with diversity within unity. The Old Testament people of God had foreigners living in their midst. They were to be treated with grace equal to the Israelites. Israel's life was not only ordered by priests but also by kings and prophets.

In the New Testament, the church of the early pages of the book of Acts was different from the Pauline house churches, and yet both were the body of Christ, the community of faith. Diversity characterized the composition of the churches of early Christianity. Jews and Gentiles, women and men, slaves and freemen found a unity in Christ through the Holy Spirit around a common Eucharistic meal. And unity and diversity is the vision of the eschatological future: people from all nations and tongues celebrating the Lamb of God.

In all the work of faith in church and in society, a dull uniformity must be resisted and a colorful diversity is to be embraced.

Reflection: "The man who eats anything must not look down on him who does not . . . for God has accepted him" (Romans 14:3).

83

The Witness of Early Christianity

Following in the Footsteps of the Martyrs

While we need to be very careful that we do not over-idealize the early Christians and turn them all into plaster saints, we are deeply challenged by the vibrancy of their faith, the depth of their love, the passion of their commitment and the extent of their service. The challenge for us is to rediscover such passion in our time.

There are more Christians in the world today than ever before. And Christianity has grown, particularly in the Third World. But proportional to the world's population increase, the percentage of Christians in the world has not increased in the last one hundred years.

Moreover, the Christian world has become strangely divided: a weakened Christianity with great prosperity in the Western world and a growing Christianity in a world of poverty in the Third World.

The faith of the early Christians brings a challenge to both the West and the Third World. To the West comes the challenge to recapture the depth of faith and commitment of the early Christians. There is also the challenge to live more sacrificially in relation to our Third World brothers and sisters. And to the Third World comes the challenge to continue to live in faith and hope in the midst of deprivation and poverty.

Martin Luther King was convinced that we need this renewal

of the gospel and that we need to recapture the vision of "these strange people, intoxicated with the wine of God's grace, [who] continued to proclaim the gospel until even men and women in Caesar's household were convinced, until jailers dropped their keys and until kings trembled on their thrones."[83] To recapture such a vision requires a new Pentecost. For it was in the power of the Spirit that the early Christians loved God, formed community, performed healings and brought the message of hope to a needy world.

Reflection: "After they prayed, the place where they were meeting was shaken. And they were all filled with the Holy Spirit and spoke the word of God boldly" (Acts 4:31).

84

The Giving of One's All

In the Service of Christ for the World

We live in a world where the first question seems to be: What is in it for me? This self-preoccupation has also begun to characterize Christians in the West. The gospel calls us in a very different direction. We are invited to be with Christ through the Holy Spirit and to live in obedience to him for the sake of the world.

Martin Luther King was only too aware that a great cause required great sacrifice. And so he called African-Americans to the cause of civil rights and to throw off centuries of oppression and marginalization. His frequent refrain was to the point: "This is no day to pay lip service to integration, we pay *life* service to it."[84] This call to commitment can be applied to any area of life, that calls for the work of justice and transformation.

To work for change is not the work of the few heroes or heroines. It is the work of many who are willing to give their all. The call to follow Christ is a call to give our all. As Christ gave himself for us by his death on a cross, so we are blessed by his sacrificial giving of himself and are called to give him our life in love, obedience and service.

To give ourselves to the cause of Christ does not mean that we simply give ourselves to spiritual or heavenly matters. Christ gave himself for this world; he was the Man for others, and so we must be. Therefore, in the fellowship of Christ and for the sake of the kingdom of God, we are called, we are invited, we are drawn in by the Spirit to give our lives in the service of Christ the King for the sake of the world.

That service may be worked out in families or in the halls of power, in a life of prayer or a life in politics, in evangelism or social transformation, in asceticism or business. In giving ourselves to Christ, nothing that we do for him and in him is small. It is great because it is for the King of peace and the God of mercy and justice.

Reflection: "As you sent me [Jesus] into the world, I have sent them into the world" (John 17:18).

85

Harmony

The Peaceful Fruit of Unity in Diversity

One of the tragedies of any form of fundamentalism, including religious fundamentalism, is that it seeks to fit our round world into a square box. It's the attempt to take the complexity of our world and to flatten it out into a dull predictability. It's the attempt to make truth a formula and to make mystery into a proposition.

Fundamentalists, including religious fundamentalists, have a desire and an agenda to reduce a complex world and the rich tapestry of faith to monochrome predictability. This is to attempt to pin down truth and to define who is inside and who is outside the box.

The biblical story is surprisingly different in its basic orientation. There we meet the God of surprises who sets slaves free, forgives sinners and invites outsiders to the feast. This amazing story calls us to understand God, but also to love, worship and serve him. This is a journey of faith seeking understanding.

The rich tapestry of faith invites us to the politics of embrace, not of exclusion. It seeks to build the community of faith in the unity of Christ and the Holy Spirit while celebrating human diversity. Martin Luther King's vision is appropriate here. He believed that the life-giving impulses in the church and the world have to do with "a creative synthesis of opposites in fruitful harmony."[85]

This is not an attempt to mingle truth and error. Rather, it is the attempt in the wide space of truth to make a place for blacks and whites, women and men, Third Worlders and Westerners to contribute to building the community of faith and the general human community. This synthesis draws together prayer and action, contemplation and service, and the works of soul-winning and community transformation. This synthesis builds diverse communities of faith to the glory of God as a witness to the world that barriers can be broken down in the love of Christ.

Reflection: "How good and pleasant it is when brothers live together in unity! It is like precious oil poured on the head, running down on the beard, running down on Aaron's beard, down upon the collar of his robes. It is as if the dew of Hermon were falling on Mount Zion. For there the LORD bestows his blessing, even life forevermore" (Psalm 133:1–3).

86

Soul Force

The Power of Nonviolent Resistance

Jesus advocated turning the other cheek and spoke of forgiving enemies. Gandhi and King applied these basic ideas to the social and public realm in the strategy of nonviolent resistance. This strategy uses peaceful means to protest injustice. It seeks to win over those in power through the example of resisting unjust laws, but being willing to be punished by those upholding such laws.

The church has succumbed at times to the use of force. And in this perverted way of gaining converts and having an influence, the church has sowed the seeds of discord and bitterness rather than the fruit of peace. The way of the church in the world, however, should never be characterized by worldly means. Instead it should be marked by the Cross through a persuasion of humility that calls for repentance.

The power of the church in the world should be the power of witness and service. It expresses the power of love and the power of forgiveness. In the social realm this witness of the church can be expressed in nonviolent resistance, where people stand up for a cause that calls for change and transformation.

Martin Luther King lays bare the heart of this strategy. It is the force of peaceful love that says no to injustice in the face of those who wish to maintain the status quo. King suggests that those who walk this peaceful road "will meet your physical force with soul force."[86] This soul force is the power of conviction and the power of love, which seeks to transform the intransigence of those in power who perpetuate injustice.

This is no cheap strategy. It is one that calls for hope and courage to make one's voice heard in the face of evil. And it seeks the conversion of the oppressor rather than his or her punishment.

Reflection: "Here is my servant, whom I uphold, my chosen one in whom I delight; I will put my Spirit on him and he will bring justice to the nations. He will not shout or cry out, or raise his voice in the streets. A bruised reed he will not break, and a smoldering wick he will not snuff out. In faithfulness he will bring forth justice; he will not falter or be discouraged till he establishes justice on earth. In his law the islands will put their hope" (Isaiah 42:1–4).

87

Discontent

A Restless Seeking for Justice

It is inappropriate for those who have enough or even have much to be marked by discontent. Sadly, this is often the case. In the West we live in a culture of complaint. Those who have much seem never to be satisfied. But it is appropriate for those who experience injustice and marginalization to express discontent. Discontent may be the first restless impulse toward liberation.

In some Christian circles, there is the strange idea that one should always be thankful no matter what the circumstances. This is not a biblical concept. While we are invited to be grateful and thankful in times of plenty and scarcity, we are never called in the biblical story to be thankful for oppression. The Hebrew slaves were not called to be thankful for their Egyptian captivity and slavery.

Martin Luther King clearly makes the point: "Discontent is sound and healthy . . . hate is always tragic."[87] The reason discontent may be healthy is because it may signal the first crack in an oppressive social reality.

Those who are poor, marginalized and oppressed are frequently told, "This is just the way things are." This is their state of life. African-American slaves in the American story were told that this was to be their lives' circumstance. Some were told that this was their God-chosen destiny. They were chosen to serve whites. And this was God's will. When the ideology of oppression is coupled with the experience of oppression, and this is further coupled with the internalization of one's situation, then indeed oppression's dark night is without light.

Discontent may be the first glimmer of light. It may lead to a growing hope that things could be different. And hope may lead to an emerging vision of what is possible. To say to the oppressed that they should not be discontent is to condemn them to the dark night of subexistence. Rather, discontent is the harbinger of hope.

Reflection: "Out of the depths I cry to you, O LORD; *O Lord, hear my voice. Let your ears be attentive to my cry for mercy" (Psalm 130:1–2).*

88

National Repentance

RETURNING TO GOD IN REPENTANCE AND FAITH

In the biblical story, there is a persistent emphasis on the repentance of individuals. It was David who repented of his sin and Zacchaeus who pledged restoration to those he had cheated. But the biblical story also knows of the conversion of Nineveh and the national repentance of Israel. The call to a nation to change its ways is an appropriate prophetic challenge even in our day.

Martin Luther King always believed that God had a purpose not only for individuals but also for the American nation as a whole. He believed that if the United States would return to its founding vision, would practice justice for its minority peoples, and would serve the world community in humility and with care, then God would use the nation for his purposes.

It is within this framework that King issued his prophetic challenge: "You have trampled over sixteen million of your brothers [African-Americans] . . . [but] if you will come to yourself and rise up and decide to come back home, I [God] will take you in."[88] It is important to note that the promise in this contemporary prophecy has nothing to do with wealth and power. The call to care for the needy and to practice love and mercy is not a call that will then make us great. No, such a call will simply make us God's beloved. The promise of the fruit of repentance is the promise of homecoming.

So often prophecy is misused and is constructed on faulty premises. So often the impression is given that service to the poor will then make us great. But this is a misunderstanding of the nature of prophecy and the purpose of service. Prophecy is a call to an alignment with God's righteousness. And service involves the way of suffering, not the way of self-glorification. Prophecy has in view the ushering in of the shalom of God, and this involves the lifting up of the poor and needy. Thus prophecy calls us to greater service, not to greater power.

Reflection: "At that time I will deal with all who oppressed you; I will rescue the lame and gather those who have been scattered. I will give them praise and honor in every land where they were put to shame. At that time I will gather you; at that time I will bring you home" (Zephaniah 3:19–20).

89

Creative Love

Building the New Out of the Ashes of the Old

Love is probably one of the most sentimentalized words in the English language. And it is hard to know what people mean when they say, "I love you." The only way to know what is meant is to see what actions accompany these words. "I love you" must be framed in expressions of care.

Martin Luther King understood that the difficult work of social change is not best done out of sheer reaction or anger and bitterness. It is best done in love. He wrote, "*Agape* is not a weak, passive love. It is love in action. *Agape* is love seeking to preserve and create community."[89]

Love is the most potent and transformative force in the world. Love not only brings about changes but—unlike the power of hatred, which leaves in its wake the flotsam of its negativity—it brings with it a peaceable kingdom, a kingdom of grace.

Love is also never a matter of words alone. Love acts. It mobilizes. It works for change, seeks justice, builds the new. Love works for what is good, not only for the few but for all. Love has the blessing of all in view.

King believed that the work of racial integration was the work of love that builds community. He believed that life together—the building of the beloved community based on justice and equality, and framed in love—was a form of life that would bless both whites and blacks. He believed that humans need each other. And he believed that the God-given diversity of our world was a gift we should responsibly utilize by building communities of inclusion and harmony. Embrace rather than exclusion is the way of love.

To exclude others is based on the politics of fear. To include others is based on the dynamics of a love that seeks the better way, the way of suffering and service.

Fear divides. It is anti-community. It seeks to protect the few or the many against others. Love unites. It draws all in its orbit. Love is the embrace of mutuality.

Reflection: "For he himself is our peace, who has made the two one and has destroyed the barrier, the dividing wall of hostility" (Ephesians 2:14).

90

Human Responsibility

Living the Good; Resisting Evil

In the biblical story, God is the central figure. But humans are blessed with dignity and responsibility. Their grand task is the continuance of the human community and to care for each other and the world. This responsibility is to be carried out under God's blessing. Sadly, many have neglected God. Others resist God. And frequently all of us do less than God's good in our world.

Human beings are capable of doing amazing things. We have built an astonishingly civilized world with its great cities and its complex infrastructures. With music, art and literature we have qualitatively enriched the human community. And in a variety of ways we have created structures of common concern and care.

So much is good in our world, and this calls for celebration and gratitude. But it is disturbing that the goodness and beauty of our world is increasingly experienced by the few rather than the many. Many experience merely the leftovers in a world of plenty.

Martin Luther King points out that "much of the evil which we experience is caused by [human] folly and ignorance and also by the misuse of . . . freedom."[90] This is true. We do sin through lack of forethought. And we do things without realizing the unfortunate consequences for others.

But this is only part of the story. We are also willfully selfish and self-protective. We do things to favor ourselves. And we ride roughshod over others, or we deliberately ignore the needs of others. What is disconcerting about all this is that in neglecting or harming others, we also harm ourselves. And we distort the very nature of what God has called us to be.

The biblical vision of the human community is one in which we are all under the blessing of God and are responsible to care for one another. Even the least is to be embraced.

Reflection: "Do not deprive the alien or the fatherless of justice . . . . Remember that you were slaves in Egypt and the LORD your God redeemed you from there. That is why I command you to do this" (Deuteronomy 24:17–18).

91

Shaping Life

Making Something Good Out of What Has Been Given

Much has been given to us: the created world, the human community, our social institutions, our families, the community of faith. But this ordering of the human community is seldom fully the way it should be. Therefore, there is the challenge to reform, to revive and revitalize, and to transform so that our world will more fully reflect God's shalom.

Some people wish to suggest that the world is just the way it should be. Such persons are usually ultraconservatives and are not those suffering poverty and oppression. Most people, including most Christians, recognize that ongoing change is called for in our world. And the most obvious reason for this is the injustice we see all around us. When the 20 percent of the rich of this world (mainly in the West) have over 80 percent of the world's riches, this does not leave much for the rest of humanity.

For Christians there are not only pragmatic reasons for the call to change but also theological ones. Christians recognize the beauty of creation but also the fallenness of humanity. And they proclaim the need for God's redemption and restoration. Thus Christians are committed to bringing about change in our world so that the world will more fully reflect God's glory.

Martin Luther King has pointed out that "existence is the

raw material out of which all life must be created."[91] Thus we have a responsibility to shape our world and the social order. This includes creating racial harmony.

Consequently, life is both a gift and a responsibility. In the gifts of creation much has been given, but in the social order much has become distorted. And so we are called to pray and to work, that God's glory will be more fully evidenced in our world.

Distortions may appear as fractures in every sphere of life, whether that be family, church, politics, or major social institutions. There is no sphere of life that is not affected by sin and that is not distorted to some extent. Thus Christians and all people of goodwill must be discerning and vigilant. They must be willing to raise a prophetic voice and then commit themselves to the hard work of social transformation.

Reflection: "God blessed them and said to them, 'Be fruitful and increase in number; fill the earth and subdue it. Rule over the fish of the sea and the birds of the air and over every living creature that moves on the ground'" (Genesis 1:28).

92

In the Face of Jesus Christ

The Mystery of God Revealed in Christ

Many religions operate on a movement of ascendancy: the human being reaching up toward the mysterious God. Christianity moves in the opposite direction, that of the Incarnation. God has come among us and has revealed his nature in the person and work of Jesus Christ. In this spiritual vision God comes down to embrace us.

In his work of racial reconciliation and integration, Martin Luther King was moved by a theological vision. He believed not only in the providential purposes of God in history bringing about change and transformation, but more particularly in the purposes of God in Christ. King wrote, "If we are to know what God is like and understand his purposes for [humankind], we must turn to Christ."[92]

There are two important dimensions to what King is saying. The first is that in Christ we know who God is. And second, it is through Christ that we can most fully know how God has acted in history. It is this latter point I wish to explore further.

The way that Christ lived his life and the way he acted as the Servant of Yahweh gives us important clues regarding the way in which we are to act in the world. What first stands out is that Christ did not operate in the world on the basis of privilege. Though he was the divine Son of God, he laid all aside to become a servant of the reign of God. We are invited to do the same—to lay aside our status and to serve others.

Second, Christ's way in the world was one of love, forgiveness and service. Jesus did not come demanding, but forgiving. His way was grace, not legalism.

Third, Jesus was the servant of the peaceable kingdom. His was not the way of force, coercion, or the misuse of power. Instead, Christ's way was one of healing love. This too is to be our way in the world.

Finally, Christ broke the power of unhealthy traditions and forged a new way of being the human community. In this community *all* were one and *all* were included.

There is little doubt that King was inspired by this vision to bring about racial equality and social change. We are to be shaped by this same vision of Christ.

Reflection: "So he [Jesus] replied to the messengers, 'Go back and report to John what you have seen and heard: The blind receive sight, the lame walk, those who have leprosy are cured, the deaf hear, the dead are raised, and the good news is preached to the poor'" (Luke 7:22).

93

Taking a Stand

Resisting Evil; Promoting the Good

One's most basic stance in the world is first of all not to be an activist, but a contemplative. We are called to the task of discernment before we are called to the responsibilities of service. We must first be the discerners of our time before we can engage the world in loving and responsible action.

Christian presence in the world can take many forms. One is the corporate presence of Christians through the church and through church-initiated institutions such as schools, colleges, hospitals and welfare services. Another form of Christian presence is through a myriad parachurch organizations, religious orders and intentional communities. Christian families are another form of Christian presence in the world, as are Christians in the workplace seeking to be salt, leaven and light for the sake of the kingdom of God.

Whatever form Christian presence may take, this presence is to be distinctive in that it is to reflect the gospel rather than the values of the world. This calls for careful discernment. Christians are to ask what is the good in our world that needs strengthening, and what is the evil that needs to be resisted, subverted and transformed.

Martin Luther King suggests that "non-cooperation with evil is as much a moral obligation as is cooperation with good."[93]

What this means is that Christians may never withdraw from the world to live in a "holy huddle." Their active participation in the world is constantly called for. But this participation cannot be mere activism. It is to be service borne out of prayer. It is action that flows from contemplation.

To discern what is good or evil requires the eye of faith, a mind of wisdom and a heart of compassion. This discernment must be a corporate discernment of the community of faith. And it can spring only from those who are already serving in the midst of life, but are actively seeking the presence of God in all things.

Reflection: "For you were once darkness, but now you are light in the Lord. Live as children of light" (Ephesians 5:8).

94

Daily Work

Doing All to the Glory of God

It is rather easy for those with meaningful employment to extol the virtues of work. But there is also work that is demeaning. And much of this work is done by ethnic minorities and the poor. While people should be encouraged to move to more purposeful work, in the final analysis we also need to find dignity in the most basic of tasks. Cleaning houses can be done to the glory of God.

In his speeches and protests and programs, Martin Luther King had African-Americans in view. But a wider audience was also in his purview. He had the silent white majority in view, as well as the poor of all strata of society and those in the Third World experiencing newfound freedoms.

But as an educated and privileged person, King particularly had the ordinary person in view: the "nobody" he encouraged to be "somebody." In this regard, he had the following to say: "No work is insignificant. If a [person] is called to be a street sweeper, he [or she] should sweep streets even as Michelangelo painted, or Beethoven composed music, or Shakespeare wrote poetry. He [or she] should sweep streets so well that all the host of heaven and earth will pause to say, 'Here lived a great sweeper who did his [or her] job well.'"[94]

Clearly this piece of pastoral advice is not meant to say to a person, "Only sweep streets, and don't try to educate yourself further, or don't try to gain other work." Nor does this suggest that every kind of work is qualitatively the same. This advice has something else in view.

Pushing the example back to earlier times, African-Americans working in the cotton fields were as much in the eye and heart of God as plantation owners. And so is the street sweeper, or the garbage collector, or the ethnic house help. Knowing that one is in the eye and heart of God is more foundational to one's dignity and humanity than being some famous person in the eyes of society. And knowing this means that I can do very "ordinary" work, including cooking or cleaning. All that I do can be done to the glory of God.

Reflection: "So whether you eat or drink or whatever you do, do it all for the glory of God" (1 Corinthians 10:31).

95

The Inner Life

A Spacious Place of Worship, Silence and Wonder

In modernity, our inner world has become a most neglected place. Our orientation is toward the outward. It has to do with our achievements, productivity and status. In living life with such a focus, not only is our inner life neglected, it is sacrificed. Thus we sacrifice what should be safeguarded and nurtured.

Martin Luther King shares our concern that we have turned things the wrong way around. We have replaced the eternal with the temporal. We have elevated work over prayer. And as King concluded in a sermon, "We have foolishly minimized the internal of our lives and maximized the external."[95]

In making these observations, I am not advocating the old dualisms of the religious world, which elevates the soul over the body, the spiritual over the material, and prayer over work. A healthy biblical spirituality emphasizes both. All of life is to be lived to the glory of God.

But our contemporary world has swung the pendulum to the other extreme. The claim is that God is no longer present to the world, and the world is no longer present to God. But we are to be encouraged to build our inner lives as much as our careers, and to form our inner-scapes as much as our urban-scapes.

Our inner world of love, imagination and hope should not simply be exploited to serve our outward activities. Our inner world may also be a world of contemplation and wonderment. The inner musings of the heart need not only burst out in music or song. We may also fall into silence. The inner world is not only the reservoir for our outward busyness. It may also be the world of worship—the world of communion with the God who has created us, but who also holds us in the intimacy of his love and grace.

Nurturing the inner life is an invitation to be present to God and to ourselves. It is the call to be playfully absent to the world's agenda.

Reflection: "I will meditate on all your works and consider all your mighty deeds. Your ways, O God, are holy. What God is so great as our God?" (Psalm 77:12–13).

96

Ideas, but Lacking Praxis

Combining Head, Heart and Hand

It's a sad and unfortunate reality. There are those hard at work responding to human need, but are devoid of creative ideas. There are those full of good ideas who never get their hands "dirty." What we need in our world are people committed to orthodoxy (right belief) and orthopraxy (right practice), as well as those imbued with orthopathy (right passion or motivation).

Martin Luther King was concerned in his day about armchair intellectuals full of great ideas but not willing to put their lives on the line. He wrote, "They are brilliant people; often they do an excellent job in developing their inner powers; but they live as if nobody else lived in the world but themselves."[96]

Armchair intellectuals may also be the armchair theologians. In comfortable, tenured positions and living well-to-do lifestyles, producing large intellectual tomes for the guild, these scholars no longer have the world, the church and the university in view in their scholarly deliberations. And if they do, it is from a safe distance created by their academic careers.

But the more fruitful thinking cannot occur in our own safety zones. It must occur in the midst of all the messiness, ambiguity, beauty and pain of life and of our world. All scholarship, including Christian theological reflection, has to do with our embeddedness in the world. And more particularly from a Christian perspective, it has to do with incarnational realities and mission.

If Jesus is the Word made flesh, then we too need to become an embodied word for the world. This embodiment must take the form of a worldly engagement that washes the feet of the world. The old Greek idea that elevates thinking over doing, ideas over deeds, is an idea that is missing from the pages of the biblical story. The God of the Bible is no mere thinker, but a God who creates, redeems, heals and renews.

Those whose ideas have never been tested in fires of practical service hold ideas that do violence to the Word made flesh.

> *Reflection: "But someone will say, 'You have faith; I have deeds.' Show me your faith without deeds, and I will show you my faith by what I do" (James 2:18).*

97

Misuse

Using Others for Our Own Gain

However difficult it may sound, we need to recognize the human propensity to make use of people to benefit ourselves. We all can be exploitative in fundamental ways. As such, we treat the other as an It rather than a Thou. In treating people in this way we do fundamental violence to the importance of loving and caring relationships and the call to bless others.

With a crystal clarity, Martin Luther King identifies this human trait of using others: "The hardhearted person never truly loves. He [or she] engages in a crass utilitarianism which values other people mainly according to their usefulness."[97] We see this problem writ large in our contemporary culture. Those who are no longer productive in the society are soon marginalized. Those who fail to maintain the pace in the workplace are soon made redundant. Those who no longer please their spouses are soon divorced. Sadly, functionality and effectiveness have also become a part of the ethos of the Western church. Pastors who produce growing numbers of church members are sought after.

But people cannot be valued only on the basis of their productivity and effectiveness. And people are not simply cogs in the big wheel. Nor are people simply to be used for some cause or so-called greater good. People also need to be celebrated for who they are. Sometimes their presence is enough.

And what of those who have not much to give? What of those who cannot make a great contribution? People are not means to certain ends. People are to be loved and appreciated for who they are, not simply for what they do.

This vision of the human being opens up space for the weary, the wounded and the disabled in the community of faith. It opens space for all of us, for not all of us can give all the time. We too need to be carried at times.

Reflection: "We who are strong ought to bear with the failings of the weak and not to please ourselves. Each of us should please his neighbor for his good, to build him up" (Romans 15:1–2).

98

Coming to Faith

God's Mysterious and Different Way with Us

In some Christian circles, coming to faith has been reduced to a certain form of decisionism. This is then regarded as a formula. But in God's wide scheme of things, there are no formulas. Peter's coming to faith was not the same as Paul's, and Augustine's conversion was not the same as John Wesley's. God works in each of us with a wide and colorful faithfulness.

Martin Luther King does not seem to have come to faith in the way I did. His was a gradual unfolding of the life of Christ within him, while mine was more dramatic. But this doesn't matter. King speaks about his own experience as follows: "Even though I have never had an abrupt conversion experience, religion has been real to me and closely knitted to life."[98] Of course, he is speaking about the Christian religion and his relationship with Christ. But what is important in this disclosure is not the first part, but the latter. What is important is not the way in which we come to faith—which may be gradual or sudden—but the impact of that faith in our lives.

For some, this impact seems to be temporary. They have a religious experience, but the experience fades and their life of relationship with God disappears. For others, the impact seems to be more peripheral to their lives. The grace of Christ is embraced, but the lordship of Christ is not lived out. Their normal life goes on with Christ as the happy extra dimension.

This appears not to have been the case with King. He speaks of faith being intrinsic to his very life. And so it should be. Faith in Christ is not a mere addendum to one's life. It is a revolution. Christ through the Spirit lives at the core of who we are, not in the attic or basement. This means that the grace of Christ and the life that Christ lived become normative and key to who we are and to the way we live in the world. At the heart of all this is that we want to serve the way Christ did.

Reflection: "To this you were called, because Christ suffered for you, leaving you an example, that you should follow in his steps" (1 Peter 2:21).

99

Torn

Doing All to the Glory of God

In the biblical story, the human being is the crown of God's creative activity. Made in God's image and endowed with great powers, the human being was given the task of caring for and shaping the created world. But this is only part of the story. The other part is that the human being became distorted and this had implications for all humans. But there is more to this part of the story as well. God's redemption can overcome every kind of distortion.

Martin Luther King grew up in a world of racial segregation. He later remembered times when he was made to feel like a nobody. He thus knew from an early age the distortion in the social fabric of society. This he later set out to rectify.

But King also understood the reality of the distortion within the human person. He writes that one's "existential situation is a state of estrangement from [one's] essential nature."[99] When we seek to understand what this internal estrangement is all about, we note several important dimensions.

The most basic dimension is becoming estranged from God at the center of our existence. We were made for fellowship, companionship and at-onement with God. The whole of our internal and external existence was to be infused with God's presence. The loss of this presence, due to human sin, puts the whole of life in a tailspin.

This results in an internal disorder. Thus the human being is at loggerheads with himself or herself. There is no abiding center, only a restless searching for one. There is no peace, only a hope that it may be found. And sadly, the human being acts in ways that bring this disorder into our social world.

Self-rectification, while a noble ideal, is no final solution, as the tale of history ceaselessly reiterates. It is only the transforming and healing love of God that can make us whole. This internal renewal can spill over into the fragility and chaos of our social world so that all may be made whole.

Reflection: "Do not offer the parts of your body to sin, as instruments of wickedness, but rather offer yourselves to God, as those who have been brought from death to life; and offer the parts of your body to him as instruments of righteousness" (Romans 6:13).

100

Beyond Rhetoric

The Joy of Embodying Our Words

We live in a world that is tired of words. So much has been said. So much has been promised, particularly by our political leaders and the masters of commerce. The priests of religion have also promised much and have left us in the wasteland of our fears. Maybe the prophets and poets can point the way forward.

Words are important. We are linguistic creatures and make sense of our world through words. We appropriate and define our world through language.

Words can describe. They can also distort. They can also open up a world of possibilities. Thus words are meant to carry us forward. And this forward movement cannot be in more words but in deeds that make the word more concrete and visible.

In one of his sermons, Martin Luther King makes the observation that "one of the great tragedies of life is that [people] seldom bridge the gulf between practice and profession."[100] Or to put that differently, they fail to bridge the divide between rhetoric and praxis, word and deed.

While Christians make much of the Bible as the Word of God, they must not forget that the Scriptures reflect a God of word and deed. In fact, God's word is deed. In creation the word brings all things into being. And in the Incarnation the

Word becomes flesh in the person of Jesus Christ, the Savior of the world.

As Christians we are called not only to share the Word of God with others, but also to embody the Word in our own lives. The church, the community of faith, is to be a hermeneutic of the gospel, an interpreter of the gospel by being a living representation of the gospel. As doers of the Word, we make the Word visible. Thus by practicing forgiveness, we make the word of forgiveness realizable. By doing the deeds of love, love becomes concrete and visible in our world.

Jesus spoke and lived the reality of love and forgiveness. He spoke of peace and was the great peacemaker. We are called to follow in his footsteps.

Reflection: "But if anyone obeys his word, God's love is truly made complete in him. This is how we know we are in him: Whoever claims to live in him must walk as Jesus did" (1 John 2:5–6).

101

God at the Center

Seeking the God Who Seeks to Be Found

There is a great mystery in the meeting between God and the human being. In the encounter where we know that God knows us, we come home to the heart of God. This is a time of disclosure and embrace. It is the mysterious work of God, who seeks to be found, and the human response of faith in the God who welcomes us.

Martin Luther King rightly emphasizes one side of the equation. As a preacher, he exhorts us to seek God, exclaiming, "So I say to you, seek God and discover him and make him a power in your life."[101] This is most appropriate. Throughout the biblical story we are invited to seek God while he may be found. This is the work of the hungry heart. It is the heart that knows its need and knows that, with God's help, healing can be found.

There are myriad ways that a heart becomes a hungry and seeking heart. It may be failure. It may be loss. But more fundamentally, a hungry heart is a heart touched by the Spirit of God awakening, drawing and beckoning.

King's exhortation is not simply to know God but for God to be a transformative presence in one's life. He invites us to know the power of God that makes us whole and that empowers us for service.

Our personal welcome by God and the joy of living in God's

presence is never meant to be a blessing only for ourselves. The goodness that works in us is to be extended to others. This means that we are called to be a healing and prophetic presence in our world. Linked to God by his grace and Spirit, we are invited to do the work of God in our world. And that work, which involves witness and care, also involves the difficult work of social transformation.

Christians live in the belief that God is at work in our society and that we are called to cooperate with him in responding to isolation, abuse of power, poverty and the scourge of injustice.

Reflection: "Seek the LORD while he may be found; call on him while he is near. Let the wicked forsake his way and the evil man his thoughts. Let him turn to the LORD, and he will have mercy on him, and to our God, for he will freely pardon" (Isaiah 55:6–7).

102

Embodiment

The Word in Us Becoming Flesh

Ours has become an age of cynicism. We have great doubts about leaders, and we are skeptical about the intent of major institutions. We gain knowledge but doubt its applicability, and in our having much we wonder why happiness eludes us. There is an urgent need for a new way to be found—the way of the Word made flesh.

I have spent a good part of my life in higher education, and I have met many fine people there. But I have also met cynical lecturers. Knowledge for them is a linguistic game, not the way to wisdom.

What we urgently need is a different kind of leader and a different kind of relationship between leaders and people. Leaders need to be more than the bearers of the word. Their task is to articulate, to explain and to expound a vision. But their task is also to mobilize, to incite people to involvement and to action.

To do this effectively, they must also be bearers of the deed, not only of the word. They must embody the word, and the vision must become flesh and blood in them. Martin Luther King puts this well: "People are often led to causes and often become committed to great ideas through persons who personify those ideas. They have to find the embodiment of the idea in flesh and blood in order to commit themselves to it."[102]

King attempted to do this. He marched. He went to jail. He

was manhandled. His house was bombed. He was killed in the midst of the cause for justice. Not only does the world cry out for such leaders, the church desperately needs them as well.

The church has become the bastion of middle-class mediocrity. And its leaders are often the priests of generality and non-engagement. Where are the leaders who are raising their voices against the materialism, racism, militarism, nationalism and hedonism of our time? And where are the leaders who are living against these false values in creative response to the vision of God's upside-down kingdom?

Reflection: "Jesus called them together and said, 'You know that the rulers of the Gentiles lord it over them, and their high officials exercise authority over them. Not so with you. Instead, whoever wants to become great among you must be your servant, and whoever wants to be first must be your slave—just as the Son of Man did not come to be served, but to serve, and to give his life as a ransom for many'" (Matthew 20:25–28).

103

Self-Reflection

THE PAINFUL WORK OF INNER INTERROGATION

Every leader needs to be sure of the direction in which he or she is taking others. This responsibility weighs heavily on every responsible leader. But this certainty of purpose and direction does not usually fall weightless from the heavens. It is usually forged in the midst of life and comes out of the fires of self-interrogation.

Leadership is usually no light task. It is often the opposite: a heavy—and at times crushing—burden. And at the heart of this weight lies the burden of discernment. Have I understood the problems and issues well? Have I set out appropriate solutions? Am I going about the task of working for change in helpful and constructive ways? These are but a few questions of purgation. There are many others.

Martin Luther King was no exception to the machinations of this difficult internal process. He said, "I subject myself to self-purification and to endless self-analysis: I question and soul search constantly into myself to be as certain as I can that I am fulfilling the true meaning of my work."[103]

This important and difficult inner task is inevitable for the healthy leader. The unhealthy leader, of course, thinks this is not necessary. Such leaders simply assume that they are always right.

But inner talk can be circular talk. It can also be blinded

talk. Hence such talk should become prayer. And such talk must become the grist for mutual discernment. Every healthy leader does not lead alone. There are to be companions on the journey. Healthy leaders have advisers and spiritual directors, and thus the pressing and often-desperate inner questions can be discussed in a community of co-discerners. And so the burdens are shared. The weight is weighted differently.

But even then and even so, the leader will still need to make the hard decisions. And this requires faith, hope and courage. Thus while leadership is a task and a responsibility, it is also a burden that will need to be carried with humility and courage.

Reflection: "Why are you downcast, O my soul? Why so disturbed within me? Put your hope in God, for I will yet praise him, my Savior and my God" (Psalm 42:5–6).

104

Propaganda

Resisting the Stories of the Powerful

We are indeed naive if we think that the world simply provides us with information, as if that information is objective and neutral. Much closer to the truth is that the powerful in the world are even more evangelistic than the church. Their message tells us what is good and what we need. We need to learn to see this as being propaganda.

When we think about the use of power, we readily think about brute power: the power of a powerful person or a nation in terms of its economic and military power. But there are many other forms of power, both good and bad.

One form of power that can be used for good or ill is informational power. Some have access to all the information regarding a controversial incident, the value or otherwise of a product, or the benefits or otherwise of a diplomatic move. Most of us get to hear only part of the story. What this is all about is that the powerful also have powerful means to tell us what they want us to know. This means that we are being propagandized.

Where all this becomes very evident is when a minority begins to question the dominant view. Those in power will do anything they can to present this other view as unacceptable and dangerous. Just think of the way the civil rights movement was initially portrayed as undermining the good order of society.

In one of his sermons, Martin Luther King noted that we

need "to be lifted above the norms of false propaganda."[104] This is equally relevant in our day. We are daily subject to the views, opinions and ideas of the mass media. And as Christians we need to become far more critical of what we are being told.

Our dream as Christians is not the dream of nationalism, or the dream of much having, or the dream of safety and well-being. Instead it is the dream of being servants of the kingdom and following the way of Christ. Thus we need to become far more culturally critical and more attuned to God's vision of life.

Reflection: "Do not conform any longer to the pattern of this world, but be transformed by the renewing of your mind. Then you will be able to test and approve what God's will is—his good, pleasing and perfect will" (Romans 12:2).

105

Opposition

Responding to Powerful Detractors

There is no doubt that Jesus experienced opposition. He was crucified by his detractors. Every leader and every movement in history that has sought to bring about change has experienced its share of opposition. If we are serving the kingdom of God, we can expect nothing else.

In his work for racial integration, in his advocacy for the poor, and in his opposition to the Vietnam War, Martin Luther King experienced his share of opposition. He once made this pertinent observation: "The guardians of the status quo lash out with denunciation against the person or organization that they consider most responsible for the emergence of the new order."[105]

And so it is. The story of history is a mere repetition of these realities. And we need think only of John Hus, Martin Luther, John Wesley and Dietrich Bonhoeffer. But the pressing question is: What of us? Or has the church in the West become so enamored with the status quo that it has lost its prophetic voice? I think the answer to this can only be a mournful yes. The church in the West is a culturally captive church with seemingly little power to be a sign, sacrament and servant of the reign of God.

What the church seems to have forgotten is that it is not full of power first and then it significantly serves the world. Usually, the opposite is the case. It may be weak, but it is on its knees in prayer. It may not be powerful, but its heart is for the world. It may not have many resources, but it is committed to the work of justice.

The power of the church does not lie first of all in its external resources, but in its interiority, its life of prayer, meditation and discernment. Its power lies in its heartbeat. Its life lies in its heart cry.

The first call of the community of faith is not to rulership, or its kingly role under Christ, or its prophetic role in challenging the world. The first call is the priestly one, to take upon itself the sorrows of our world and to bear these in prayer to the heart of God. From this starting point, the prophetic and kingly functions of the church may well flow.

Reflection: "Let us fix our eyes on Jesus, the author and perfecter of our faith, who for the joy set before him endured the cross, scorning its shame, and sat down at the right hand of the throne of God. Consider him who endured such opposition from sinful men, so that you will not grow weary and lose heart" (Hebrews 12:2–3).

106

Indebtedness

Living Generational Thankfulness

When we are young and overly enamored with our own strength and abilities, we think that we can change the world and that we can start from a new beginning. As time goes on, we begin to realize how much of the old persists and how dependent we are on those who have gone before us and have made their contribution to society, to the church, to the arts, to literature and to the whole spectrum of human creativity.

We are all too aware of the revolutionary movements of fascism and communism that sought to radically change the modern world. Their failure partly lay in the fact that they did not radically change the modern world but repeated some of its worst features. The significant lesson in this is that usually much less changes than what we had hoped for. There is great power in tradition. And the old does persist even though it is continually threatened. The point, however, is not to maintain the old because it is old, but to maintain the good that is in the old and to seek its contemporary application.

Martin Luther King once made the observation that "we are everlasting debtors to known and unknown men and women."[106] And so we are! The present is a great storehouse of the past. We are the recipients of so much that has been given. A long heritage of ideas, values and culture has been handed on to us. And so it is with the church. The church was not born yesterday. Its more than two-thousand-year journey has produced an impact on the world and has brought to birth theologies, hymns, art, architecture and missional strategies.

We are, therefore, invited to take our place in the contemporary world as being mindful of the old and open to the new. We are to be grateful for the past and willing to lay foundations for the future. Therefore our task is not a static one. Thankful for what we have been given, we seek to be God's faithful servants in the present, so that this generation may know the works of God and glorify his majesty.

Reflection: "But from everlasting to everlasting the LORD's love is with those who fear him, and his righteousness with their children's children—with those who keep his covenant and remember to obey his precepts" (Psalm 103:17–18).

107

The God Who Is There

Seeking the Presence of God in All of Life

There are those who were nervous that the advances of science would banish God from our world. So they developed the idea of the God of the gaps. This meant that in realms where science could not penetrate, there God was located. But God cannot be confined to the periphery of our existence and of our knowledge. God is at the center.

The story of God is the story of the community of faith. No philosopher has been able to give an absolute rationale and convincing explanation for the reality of God in our world. No scientist has been able to give proof for God's existence. And despite much effort, the hard work of neither the archaeologist nor the historian can provide certitude that God has acted and continues to act in our world.

The story of God is the story of revelation to an ancient people to whom God revealed himself as the I am that I am. This unfolding story involving the ancient people of Israel is a story of faith. The continuation of this story in the person and work of Jesus Christ and in the birth of the church is also a story of faith. There are those who believed that Jesus was Messiah, was the Son of God, and was the One bringing in the reign of God, who spoke of forgiveness, healing and new life.

And so this story of revelation and faith has continued. There have been times when it has been fervently believed. At other times, the power of this story seems to have waned and people have been skeptical regarding its truth, its ability to be known and its power. In the West, now is such a time.

But Martin Luther King believed in the enduring power of this story of faith. As he said, "These new advances have banished God neither from the microcosmic compass of the atom nor from the vast, unfathomable ranges of interstellar space. . . . God is still here."[107] This is the confession of faith that ordinary women and men, philosophers, historians, scientists and artists still make. God is still here.

Reflection: "For God so loved the world that he gave his one and only Son, that whoever believes in him shall not perish but have eternal life. For God did not send his Son into the world to condemn the world, but to save the world through him" (John 3:16–17).

108

The Resurrection

The Hope of the Life to Come

There are many times when the relationship between the present and the future can be conceived of in unhelpful ways. The two extremes suggest that we only live for the present or the future. This means that one rejects future hope or one rejects the importance of how one lives in the now. The biblical vision is to live the now in the light of the future and to live the now in the hope of God's final consummation of all things.

Past, present and future are the three zones of human existence.

We seek to be attentive to the present and to live it with joy and responsibility. We see the present as God's gift of time to us, and we are thankful for the life that has been given to us and for the opportunities that come our way.

We are also to be mindful of past. The long past is the great storehouse of human wisdom and culture. The history of Christianity rooted in the tradition of Old and New Testaments is part of this long past. And the short past is the story of our individual lives up to this point in time.

Much of the long past is a living past that impacts us in the present. And the short past is the totality of who we are in the present. Both the long and short past are to be lived in the light of the future.

Christians live their lives serving God in the present but in the light of the future hope of the life to come. Their whole existence is understood not only as a now but also as a future. Thus they can live the present more daringly, knowing that the present is not the full meaning of life; the future is.

Martin Luther King once expressed this as follows: "Death is not a period that ends the great sentence of life, but a comma that punctuates it to more lofty significance."[108] We live in the hope of the resurrection and of the life to come. And in that hope we long for the full restoration of our own humanity and of all things. The mending of all creation. The restoration of all things. Fullness of life in new heavens and a new earth. And ever to live in God's presence. These are the songs of hope of the Christian.

Reflection: "So will it be with the resurrection of the dead. The body that is sown is perishable, it is raised imperishable; it is sown in dishonor, it is raised in glory; it is sown in weakness, it is raised in power; it is sown a natural body, it is raised a spiritual body" (1 Corinthians 15:42–44).

109

The Width of Life

Widening the Arteries of Human Existence

We are instinctively self-protective and much of our life revolves around our own interests and concerns. This attempt to safeguard ourselves is meant to ensure our own happiness and wellbeing. But no matter how understandable all this may be, it narrows rather than deepens and broadens our existence. True well-being also has the other in view.

Martin Luther King's adult life began as a preacher in an African-American church in America's South. His life broadened to become a national civil rights leader, a Nobel Peace Prize winner and a human rights leader on the stage of world history. King himself conceptualized this in a most fundamental way. He writes that one really lives by rising "above the narrow confines of his [or her] individualistic concerns to the broader concerns of all humanity."[109] It is obvious that not all do this in the same way. Some do become national figures. Others simply bless and influence those within their immediate circle of relationships.

The scope and width of what we do in serving others is not simply in our own hands. It is God's gift, or as some would put it, it is a matter of destiny. But the intentionality lies in our own heart and hands. In our small corner, we can begin to serve others well. We can be the servants of Christ to them. We can carry the water, bread and wine of the Spirit to them. We can bless rather than ignore, heal rather than hurt.

We never know in what ways God may take up our loaves and fishes and use these for the wider purposes of his kingdom. A neighborhood ministry may become a national movement. But the issue is not the desire to become successful and famous. The key is to serve well those within one's initial sphere of influence and to serve them radically, not being afraid of current opinions or previous strategies.

To live for Christ and for the sake of the world is to widen our narrow arteries of self-preoccupation and to enter the broad stream of the Spirit's renewing work.

Reflection: "Each of us should please his neighbor for his good, to build him up. For even Christ did not please himself but, as it is written: 'The insults of those who insult you have fallen on me'" (Romans 15:2–3).

110

Surge of Freedom

Impulse Toward the Light

Whether it occurs within our families, churches, neighborhoods, organizations, or within the entire social fabric of a nation, all forms of oppression, neglect, or marginalization will eventually be seen for what they are and will be resisted. While we may suffer the darkness long, we were made for freedom.

The Hebrew slaves in Egyptian captivity suffered long their oppression. But then they cried to Yahweh to deliver them. This story is paradigmatic. Again and again it has repeated itself. Whether it was the Moravian impulse for freedom in the late Middle Ages or the collapse of Soviet communism in the modern world, the impulse toward freedom resonates throughout the pages of history.

Martin Luther King played a key leadership role in the surge for freedom of African-Americans in the contemporary United States. He therefore speaks from personal experience as well as from history when he notes, "Oppressed people cannot remain oppressed forever. The yearning for freedom eventually manifests itself."[110] And even when it is a long time coming, it will come!

This, I believe, is true for every form of freedom. While we may primarily focus on national or economic freedom, freedom can take many forms. And the longing for spiritual freedom is part of the human heartbeat. This too will once again come, even to the Western world, which is presently plunged into spiritual darkness.

Humans will come to see that the sloganeering of our contemporary culture, with its secularism, materialism, hedonism and crass individualism, has brought bondage rather than freedom and darkness rather than light. While this secular gospel is temporarily triumphant in the Western world, its time is limited and its days are numbered.

Just as African-Americans rose up in the 1960s to claim their freedom, so too people starved of spirituality and relationally, of inner wisdom and hope, of faith and prayer will rise up again to claim new life in God's Spirit.

Reflection: "And afterward, I will pour out my Spirit on all people. Your sons and daughters will prophesy, your old men will dream dreams, your young men will see visions" (Joel 2:28).

III

Two Movements

Oppression and Freedom; Law and Grace

Life is complex. And the movement of life is never singular. It is dialectical. The very genesis of life carries the germs of death. And in the vast scope of our social reality are the movements of freedom and repression, hope and despair. The Christian life also knows this double movement. The natural and supernatural, law and grace are not juxtaposed but jostle together in the Christian experience.

We sometimes wish that it could all be very different. And so we wish for simplistic answers to complex problems. In times of difficulty, we wish that there could just be peace. Not only is life not like that, but I wonder whether we can really live well in such a singular frame. If we just have peace, where would the struggle be? If we just had joy, where would the questing be?

The human being lives with a double memory: the memory of a primordial innocence and the memory of a willful disobedience. And the human being lives in present brokenness and in the hope of God's final healing. There is nothing singular about that! It is dialectical and complex.

And so it is with all that we do. Martin Luther King puts it well: "In the midst of the upward thrust of goodness there is the downward pull of evil."[III]

In our life of prayer, there is fervency and stagnation. In our walk of faith, there is obedience and doubt. In our service to others, there is generosity and selfishness. In our work of building the community of faith, there is joy and frustration. And in building the wider community, there are signs of goodness and there are unfortunate, unintended consequences.

We don't live the Christian life on a single musical note. It is instead musically and tonally complex. Sometimes it is a beautiful melody and at other times it is a cacophony of sounds. There is nothing simplistic about any of this. But would you want to live any other way?

Reflection: "For we are to God the aroma of Christ among those who are being saved and those who are perishing. To the one we are the smell of death; to the other, the fragrance of life. And who is equal to such a task?" (2 Corinthians 2:15–16).

112

Raise Your Voice

From Worship to Thanksgiving to Advocacy

God is a God who speaks. As humans we also speak. And our speaking takes many forms: scientific and poetic, functional and romantic, secular and religious. Our speaking can be life-giving or death-dealing. But when our speaking follows the melody line of the kingdom of God, it will move from adoration to thanksgiving and from proclamation to advocacy.

Our speaking is a form of externalization. While much of our speaking is about the ordinary and daily realities of life, and these are important, we also speak of possibilities, of what may yet be. Our speaking is both the language of functionality and the language of hope.

Martin Luther King focuses our attention on the language of mission. He reminds us that "we are called to speak for the weak, for the voiceless, for victims of our nation and for those it calls enemy."[112] This speaking is important. And to this we shall return. But the language of mission must be preceded by other ways of speaking.

For the Christian the primary way of speaking is the language of adoration. We adore God for who he is and for what he has done and what he continues to do. This is the language of worship.

Adoration invites us to the language of thankfulness. We

are thankful for all the signs of God's presence and goodness among us. We are thankful for his grace, thankful for the community of faith, thankful for his Spirit among us, and thankful for all the good gifts of life that we have received.

This leads us to the language of mission and service. And here the Christian's language is one both of witness and of advocacy. In witness we speak of God's salvation. In advocacy we speak on behalf of the oppressed. King takes the language of advocacy to its ultimate expression: to speak for one's nation's enemies. This is to speak against the nation and for those the nation has demonized. This is the language that brings into collision the dimensions of civil religion and the sphere of the kingdom of God.

Reflection: "Sing to God, sing praise to his name, extol him who rides on the clouds—his name is the Lord—and rejoice before him. A father to the fatherless, a defender of widows, is God in his holy dwelling. God sets the lonely in families, he leads forth the prisoners with singing; but the rebellious live in a sun-scorched land" (Psalm 68:4–6).

113

A World House

Living in a Global Community

In so many ways we are creatures of time, habit and place. We are socialized into a particular culture and into the smaller world of our family. We thus belong to a smaller and a larger world at the same time. And in our kind of world, we are invited to expand the borders of our national identity and to become citizens of the world community.

Martin Luther King in no way merely served the interests of his family, his church, or his race. His was a vision to serve the wider community. In working for racial integration he had white persons in view as much as African-Americans. In working in the southern states of the United States, he also began to engage the issues of the northern states. And in seeking to bring about change in the whole nation, he had the whole post-colonial world also in view.

Therefore King began to speak about the global reality in which we all must live. And his famous phrase was, "We have inherited a large house, a great 'world house.'"[113] This was an invitation not only to move beyond narrow sectional interests, racism and ethnocentrism, but more importantly to move to a position of commonality and sharing. This recognition of being part of a world house is particularly relevant for Christians. They are part of a global faith and a global church. What happens to the church in Rwanda, Poland, or China should concern the Christian as much as what happens in his or her local Baptist or Roman Catholic church. This too calls for commonality and sharing.

If God has blessed us with a world house, then there is room for all. And there is enough for all. But there is not enough for all when the greed of some is insatiable. The West's share in the world house is excessive, and we will live with the emptiness of our plenty, but without God's benediction, until we make room in the world house for all those whom God desires to bless.

Reflection: "The righteous care about justice for the poor, but the wicked have no such concern" (Proverbs 29:7).

114

Children of Light

Servants of God's Kingdom, Prophets to the World

There is no doubt that an inward-looking and world-denying Christianity comes from aspects of the distorted picture of the church in history and not from the biblical story. Abraham's calling was to be a blessing to the nations. The early church's calling was to be a witness to the death and resurrection of Jesus Christ, and they were told to tell that story to the whole world.

Christians are not to be worldly. That is, they are not to be shaped by the distorted values of their culture and to live lives of unforgiveness and unrighteousness. Instead, they are to live in love, peace and forgiveness to all, including their detractors and enemies.

But Christians have everything to do with the world. They live in it. They have a priestly and prayerful responsibility for the world. And they have a prophetic role to play. They are to call the world to God's light, truth and salvation.

The Scripture uses many images and metaphors to describe our role in the world. The main ones are that we are called to be salt, leaven and light. Salt preserves. Leaven inwardly transforms. And light exposes the darkness so that the truth can shine.

Martin Luther King, however, shocks us back to reality. He writes that he is "saddened by the fears and apathy of the children of light."[114] Instead of playing the important servant role in the world to call it into the beauty and light of God's reign, Christians are frequently self-preoccupied, lacking vision and uncertain in a complex and changing world. So instead of being salt, leaven and light, they are irrelevant.

Yet this cannot be. And God cannot allow this to continue. For God's heartbeat is for the world, seeking its salvation and transformation. And God seeks for us to join him in his love and concern for the world. Thus we Christians are called to repentance and transformation. We are called to lay aside our insecurities and selfishness. We are called once again to serve Christ as Savior and Lord and to do his bidding in our world.

Reflection: "We are therefore Christ's ambassadors, as though God were making his appeal through us. We implore you on Christ's behalf: Be reconciled to God. God made him who had no sin to be sin for us, so that in him we might become the righteousness of God" (2 Corinthians 5:20–21).

115

The Mountain Top

Embracing God's Strange Purposes

It matters not in what sort of role we find ourselves; we all face difficulties, disappointments and hardships. And so we all have to face the question: How do we keep going without being overtaken by discouragement? There are many answers to this question, and people find differing resources to keep going. I believe that one of the greatest resources is a visionary experience.

Martin Luther King was constantly told by his advisers to stick to the issue of tackling racism. But he believed that he also had to respond to the issues of poverty and war. He believed that racism, economics and militarism were interrelated.

And so King worked on many fronts both nationally and internationally with signs of hope, with strides toward progress, and with many discouragements along the way. One does not easily change a world of gross inequality into a brotherhood or sisterhood of *koinonia*. And a world long scarred by the use of swords and atomic bombs does not readily walk the way of shalom. So how did King keep going?

And how do we continue to face our own challenges and responsibility?

King testifies, "We've got some difficult days ahead. But it really doesn't matter with me now. Because I've been to the mountain top."[115] While it is anybody's guess what King actually experienced—because he does not go into detail—it is clear that he had some kind of visionary experience.

I am suggesting that, while rational commitments and agreements are important to keep us focused, there is nothing so powerful as a visionary experience to propel us forward, even against great odds. In fact the odds become irrelevant to the person who has seen "the promised land."

Change agents need more than a rationale for change. They need more than a vision for change. They need to be able to see far enough down the road to know what it leads to. Leaders with such a vision cannot be stopped, no matter what the blockages or hindrances.

Reflection: "For I will take you out of the nations; I will gather you from all the countries and bring you back into your own land. I will sprinkle clean water on you, and you will be clean; I will cleanse you from all your impurities and from all your idols. I will give you a new heart and put a new spirit in you; I will remove from you your heart of stone and give you a heart of flesh" (Ezekiel 36:24–26).

116

In God

JOINED TO THE BEING AND PURPOSE OF GOD

To say that God is our true home is using metaphorical language. Homecoming is another way of explaining an encounter with God that draws us deeply into the life of God through the Holy Spirit.

All the sages and mystics have spoken about the great mystery of being found by God and living in God. And union with God has been the quest of the great writers of Christian spirituality. Martin Luther King puts it all simply when he says that the one "who loves is a participant in the being of God."[116]

It is important to note that in many Christian circles the emphasis is not on union with God, but on receiving the blessings of God. Here the focus is on receiving and enjoying the salvation that God gives. In other Christian circles the focus is not on blessings received but on service given. Here one's relationship with God is very much oriented around mission and ministry and on serving God in the world.

Both of these emphases are important. But another emphasis is equally important and should not be lost from view. This has to do with relationship and intimacy between the creature and the Creator. The focus of the mystics is to become more Godlike. This has to do with entering more fully into the presence of God and living in and by his Spirit. This is the mystery of love. Known and loved by God, we grow in our love for him and our understanding of him.

This is no pietistic experience that should become an end in itself. The more fully we live in God, the more fully we can be present to our neighbor. Love of God always spills into our horizontal relationships: family, friends, colleagues, the neighbor, the stranger, the enemy.

Reflection: "He who dwells in the shelter of the Most High will rest in the shadow of the Almighty. I will say of the L*ORD*, *'He is my refuge and my fortress, my God, in whom I trust'" (Psalm 91:1–2).*

117

The Voice of Jesus

Being Attentive to the God Who Speaks

There are many ways that God speaks to us. We are confident that Jesus Christ, the living Word, speaks to us through the written Word. The Bible is, therefore, not simply some ancient religious book. It is indeed the Word of God. But the Spirit of God also speaks to us in dreams, in preaching, through counseling, through the word of a friend or even of an enemy. May we have an attentive heart to hear!

In the pages of the Bible we everywhere hear the joyful refrain that God will never leave us or forsake us and that God is an ever-present help in times of trouble. In the midst of troubles and difficulties, however, we can become overwhelmed and lose our way. And we can become less than trusting. We may even fail to see that God is there.

In the large social causes in which he took a leadership role, Martin Luther King was at times deeply discouraged. He sometimes felt like giving up. But he kept going because he "heard the voice of Jesus saying still to fight on."[117] This undoubtedly was an inner voice. But King experienced this as the very voice of Jesus encouraging him to continue.

This should not be regarded as something strange or wildly mystical. In our human relationships we can experience an absent spouse or family member or friend as truly as one who is very close. And so we are comforted. So why should our relationship with God not be similar? Surely the God of the universe through his Spirit can draw close to us and can speak deep within our very being, bringing clarity, insight, encouragement, hope and fortitude.

God is both within and without us. God is wholly separate and wholly close. And in times of need, darkness, or despair, the presence of God can well up within us, giving us new life.

The God who is present is a God who speaks. May we have the gift of the listening heart.

> *Reflection: "He saw heaven opened and something like a large sheet being let down to earth by its four corners. It contained all kinds of four-footed animals, as well as reptiles of the earth and birds of the air. Then a voice told him, 'Get up, Peter. Kill and eat.' 'Surely not, Lord!' Peter replied. 'I have never eaten anything impure or unclean.' The voice spoke to him a second time, 'Do not call anything impure that God has made clean'" (Acts 10:11–15).*

118

God's Strong Love

Greater Than Our Weakness

In the midst of our work, whether we are serving our family, the church, a business, an educational institution, or world politics, it is easy for us to gain the idea that it all depends on us. And so we carry great burdens we were never meant to carry. It does not depend on us when we are working with God, rather than for God.

Martin Luther King expressed it well: "It is possible for me to falter; but I am profoundly secure in my knowledge that God loves us; he has not worked out a design for our failure."[118] And how true this is! Leaders are not infallible. They too have their weaknesses and their struggles. And recognizing this can be a great safeguard. Thus their hope is not in their own ability, but in what God will do.

This is how we are all called to live. And it matters not what our role and task in life may be. To trust that God is working both with us and beyond us is a source of hope and comfort. And we do need God to work beyond us. What I mean by this is that God works both through what we do, but also apart from what we do. This is to acknowledge that God is greater. We do our part, but God is the source. We do our task, but God is our inspiration. We do the work, but God blesses and multiplies the work of our hands.

What a beautiful way to live. This puts everything into a

right perspective. We are not God, so we should not attempt to do a godlike task. We are humans. We are servants of the kingdom and of the King of the kingdom, Jesus Christ our Lord. And so whatever role we are called to play, we look to God more than to ourselves.

And if what we do is all about serving the purposes of God in our time, then we can trust that we will receive God's benediction. To live this way is not to take upon ourselves more than we are called to bear.

Reflection: "But the Lord said to Ananias, 'Go! This man is my chosen instrument to carry my name before the Gentiles and their kings and before the people of Israel. I will show him how much he must suffer for my name'" (Acts 9:15–16).

119

The God Who Is Greater

Trust in the God Who Is the Sovereign Lord

We have all heard the phrase, your God is too small. This is not a comment leveled at the world, but at the church, the community of faith. The contemporary church has become defensive about the faith and has erroneously thought that the more it becomes like the world the more acceptance it will gain. This has been a grave mistake. The church needs to recover its role in pointing to the greatness and love of God.

The task of the church is not to become a repetition of the world. It is to be a small repetition of the life of Jesus. The church does need to see itself as a friend of the world and as a servant to the world, but not on the world's terms. The church's authentic existence needs to be rooted in the God who is wholly Other and yet who has drawn close to us in Jesus Christ.

This means that the people of God will always be sojourners. They are people who are out of step. They are a colony of heaven on earth. Or as one author once put it, we are too late for earth and too early for heaven. Christians are a people who live between the times: the first coming of Christ in weakness and humility, and the second coming in power and glory. And as such, they seek to live now in anticipation of the world to come.

Martin Luther King once commented, "Genuine faith imbues us with the conviction that beyond time is a divine Spirit and beyond life is Life."[119] This vision celebrates that God is greater than we and that there is more to life than the mere living of it.

True life has to do with being caught up with the vast operations of the Spirit of God in human history. And we are to concretize this in living as servants of the kingdom in our homes, neighborhoods and communities.

The vision of God's final future does not make us irrelevant to the world. But it does disconnect us from the world's agenda—all that is not of ultimate importance. Doing the will of God is.

Reflection: "For the creation was subject to frustration, not by its own choice, but by the will of the one who subjected it, in hope that the creation itself will be liberated from its bondage to decay and brought into the glorious freedom of the children of God" (Romans 8:20–21).

120

I Have a Dream

Living God's Eschatological Vision

In one sense there is nothing rational about living the Christian life. And there is nothing rational about the biblical vision. That vision of new life and transformation, and of new heavens and a new earth, is nothing but audacious. And living the Christian life is nothing short of revolutionary, because it involves the magic of God's upside-down kingdom.

Martin Luther King is famous for his "I Have a Dream" speech, in which he exclaimed, "I still have a dream that one day justice will roll down like water and righteousness like a mighty stream. . . . I still have a dream today that one day war will come to an end. . . . I still have a dream."[120]

King's vision was no personal pipe dream. It was a vision born out of his formation and shaping by the biblical story. The difference between King and many others was that he refused to relegate this vision only to the final future. He saw that this vision was also relevant for his time.

And this is precisely the challenge of faith and the power of hope. It is one thing to believe that all will be well in the afterlife. It is quite another thing to believe that God's redemptive, healing and restorative purposes are also for now. It is easy to relegate people who believe such things to the margins with comments such as, Oh, he is an idealist; or, She is hopelessly unrealistic. This means that we want and expect the sober and bitter and unjust realities of our world to continue, and to expect and work for radical change is like trying to catch the wind.

Yet that is precisely what we are called to do—to catch the wind of the Spirit. To be full of the power of God as he works his wondrous deeds in our forlorn world. To have a dream need not be wishful thinking. It can be faith and hope in what the Almighty will do.

Reflection: "'They will build houses and dwell in them; they will plant vineyards and eat their fruit . . . . They will not toil in vain or bear children doomed to misfortune; for they will be a people blessed by the L*ORD, they and their descendants with them. . . . The wolf and the lamb will feed together, and the lion will eat straw like the ox, but dust will be the serpent's food. They will neither harm nor destroy on all my holy mountain,' says the* L*ORD" (Isaiah 65:21, 23, 25).*

Appendix

A Brief Chronology of the Life of Martin Luther King Jr.

1929	Born to the Reverend and Mrs. Martin Luther King Sr. on January 15 in Atlanta, Georgia.
1935–44	Attends David T. Howard Elementary School, the Atlanta University Laboratory School and the Booker T. Washington High School.
1944–48	Attends and graduates from Morehouse College, Atlanta, with a BA in Sociology.
1947	Is licensed to preach and becomes an assistant to his father, who is pastor at Ebenezer Baptist Church, Atlanta.
1948	On February 25, King is ordained to the Baptist ministry.
1948–51	Attends Crozer Theological Seminary in Chester, Pennsylvania. Graduates with a Bachelor of Divinity degree. During this time, King becomes more interested in the work and writings of Gandhi.
1951	Enrolls in Boston University for a PhD.
1953	Marries Coretta Scott in Marion, Alabama, on June 18.
1954	The U.S. Supreme Court in the Brown vs. Board of Education case rules that racial segregation in public schools is unconstitutional.

1954	On October 31, King is installed as the twentieth pastor of Dexter Avenue Church in Montgomery.
1955	Receives a PhD in Systematic Theology from Boston University on June 5.
1955	Martin and Coretta's first child, Yolanda Denise, is born on November 17.
1955	On December 1, Mrs. Rosa Parks refuses to relinquish her bus seat to a white man and is arrested.
1955	On December 5, a bus boycott is implemented, and King is elected as the president of the newly formed Montgomery Improvement Association, which organized the boycott.
1956	A bomb is thrown on the porch of the King's home on January 30. No one is injured.
1956	On February 21, King and other leaders in the bus boycott are charged with being party to a conspiracy to hinder the operation of a bus company.
1956	A U.S. district court rules on June 4 that racial segregation on buses is unconstitutional.
1957	An unexploded bomb is discovered on the front porch of the King home on January 27.
1957	King is elected as the president of the newly founded Southern Christian Leadership Conference (SCLC).
1957	On February 18, *Time* magazine puts King on its front cover.
1957	On May 17, at the Lincoln Memorial,

	Washington, DC, King gives the speech marking the third anniversary of the Supreme Court's desegregation decision.
1957	Martin Luther III, the Kings' second child, is born on October 23.
1958	King, along with other leaders, meets President Eisenhower on June 23.
1958	King is arrested on a charge of loitering on September 3.
1958	*Stride Toward Freedom: The Montgomery Story* is published by Harper & Row.
1958	King is stabbed by Mrs. I. Curry in Harlem on September 20 while doing a book signing.
1959	Dr. and Mrs. King spend a month (February–March) in India studying Gandhi's nonviolent methods for achieving social change, as guests of Prime Minister Nehru.
1960	On January 24, the King family moves to Atlanta. Martin Luther King becomes copastor with his father at Ebenezer Baptist Church.
1960	King is arrested on February 17 on charges of tax falsification. He is acquitted some months later.
1960	King meets with presidential candidate John F. Kennedy on June 24 to discuss racial issues.
1960	King is arrested on October 19 at an Atlanta sit-in and is jailed. Charges are later dropped.
1961	Dexter Scott, the Kings' third child, is born on January 30.
1961	On May 4, the first group of Freedom Riders

	to integrate interstate buses leaves Washington, DC. The bus is burned outside Anniston, Alabama, and the Freedom Riders are beaten by a mob on arrival in Birmingham.
1961	King is arrested on December 16 at an Albany, Georgia, demonstration.
1962	King is arrested on July 27 at an Albany City Hall prayer vigil. He is jailed.
1962	King meets with President John F. Kennedy on October 16.
1963	The Kings' fourth child, Bernice Albertine, is born on March 28.
1963	King is arrested in Birmingham to protest segregation of eating facilities. On April 16, he writes his famous "Letter from Birmingham Jail."
1963	On May 20, the Supreme Court of the United States rules that Birmingham's segregation ordinances are unconstitutional.
1963	*Strength to Love* is published in June by Harper & Row.
1963	On August 28, King delivers his "I Have a Dream" speech on the steps of the Lincoln Memorial in Washington, DC, to a huge crowd of integrationist marchers.
1963	Governor George Wallace attempts to stop school integration on September 2–10 in Alabama, using state troopers.
1963	On November 22, President John F. Kennedy is assassinated in Dallas, Texas.

1964	In May and June, King joins SCLS workers in demonstrations for the integration of public accommodation in St. Augustine, Florida. He is jailed.
1964	King attends the signing into law by President Lyndon B. Johnson of the Public Accommodations Bill at the White House on July 2.
1964	Riots hit Harlem on July 18–23 and in the following month in New Jersey, Illinois and Pennsylvania.
1964	King visits West Berlin at the invitation of Mayor Willy Brandt.
1964	King has an audience with Pope Paul VI at the Vatican on September 18.
1964	King receives the Nobel Peace Prize in Oslo, Norway, on December 10.
1964	Malcolm X, leader of the Organization of Afro-American Unity, is murdered by blacks in New York on February 21.
1965	More than three thousand protest marchers leave Selma for Montgomery, Alabama. Along the way they are joined by another twenty-five thousand marchers. King addresses this crowd at the end of the march.
1965	King visits Chicago to join the SCLC and the Coordinating Council of Community Organizations for joint activities.
1965	On August 6, the 1965 Voting Rights Act is signed into law by President Johnson.

1965	In Watts, Los Angeles, racial riots rage from August 11–16, leaving thirty-five people dead.
1966	The Kings move to a black ghetto in Chicago in February and also meet with Elijah Muhammad, leader of the Nation of Islam.
1966	King reads an antiwar statement at a Washington rally to protest the Vietnam War on May 16.
1966	Stokely Carmichael publicly uses the slogan "black power" for the first time.
1966	James Meredith is shot on June 6, soon after he began his March Against Fear.
1966	King launches a campaign on July 10 to make Chicago an open city regarding housing.
1967	*Where Do We Go From Here?* is completed in January.
1967	On March 25, at the Chicago Coliseum, King attacks America's Vietnam War involvement.
1967	Rioting rages on the campus of the all-African-American Jackson State College on May 10–11.
1967	During riots in Newark, New Jersey, on July 12–17, twenty-three people are killed and over 700 are injured.
1967	Forty-three people die in the Detroit riots on July 23–30.
1967	On November 27, King announces the formation by the SCLC of a Poor People's Campaign.
1968	King leads six thousand protesters on a march

in support of sanitation workers in Memphis on March 28.

1968 King's last speech, "I've Been to the Mountain Top," is given at the Memphis Masonic Temple on April 3.

1968 King is assassinated on April 4 by a sniper while on the balcony of the Lorraine Motel, Memphis. James Earl Ray is later captured and convicted of King's murder.

Notes

1. King Jr., Martin Luther, 1981, p. 16.
2. King, Coretta Scott, 1983, p. 3.
3. King Jr., Martin Luther, 1988, p. 14.
4. Washington, J. M. (ed.), 1986, p. 263.
5. King, Coretta Scott, 1983, p. 23.
6. King Jr., Martin Luther, 1981, p. 14.
7. Washington, J. M. (ed.), 1986, p. 226.
8. King Jr., Martin Luther, 1989, p. 72.
9. King, Coretta Scott, 1983, p. 9.
10. King Jr., Martin Luther, 1989, p. 69.
11. Washington, J. M. (ed.), 1986, p. 231.
12. King Jr., Martin Luther, 1988, pp. 36–37.
13. King Jr., Martin Luther, 1989, p. 32.
14. King Jr., Martin Luther, 1981, p. 144.
15. Washington, J. M. (ed.), 1986, pp. 37–38.
16. King, Coretta Scott, 1983, p. 48.
17. King Jr., Martin Luther, 1981, p. 62.
18. Washington, J. M. (ed.), 1986, p. 20.
19. King Jr., Martin Luther, 1989, p. 74.
20. King, Coretta Scott, 1983, p. 47.
21. King Jr., Martin Luther, 1981, p. 13.
22. Washington, J. M. (ed.), 1986, p. 19.
23. King Jr., Martin Luther, 1989, p. 77.
24. King Jr., Martin Luther, 1981, p. 141.

25. King, Coretta Scott, 1983, p. 11.

26. Washington, J. M. (ed.), 1986, p. 267.

27. King Jr., Martin Luther, 1988, p. 21.

28. King Jr., Martin Luther, 1981, p. 13.

29. King, Coretta Scott, 1983, p. 9.

30. Washington, J. M. (ed.), 1986, p. 207.

31. King Jr., Martin Luther, 1968, p. 162.

32. King Jr., Martin Luther, 1964, p. 88.

33. Washington, J. M. (ed.), 1986, p. 42.

34. King Jr., Martin Luther, 1958, p. 48.

35. Quoted in Harding, V. 1996, p. 61.

36. King Jr., Martin Luther, 1958, p. 160.

37. King, Coretta Scott, 1983, p. 80.

38. Washington, J. M. (ed.), 1986, p. 40.

39. King Jr., Martin Luther, 1989, p. 64.

40. King Jr., Martin Luther, 1981, p. 111.

41. Quoted in Fairclough, A., 1995, p. 59.

42. King, Coretta Scott, 1983, p. 10.

43. Washington, J. M. (ed.), 1986, p. 241.

44. King Jr., Martin Luther, 1981, p. 133.

45. King Jr., Martin Luther, 1989, p. 59.

46. Quoted in Baldwin, L. V., 1992, p. 47.

47. Washington, J. M. (ed.), 1986, p. 280.

48. King, Coretta Scott, 1983, p. 75.

49. King Jr., Martin Luther, 1981, p. 83.

50. Quoted in Baldwin, L. V., 1991, p. 280.

51. King Jr., Martin Luther, 1958, p. 154.

52. King Jr., Martin Luther, 1981, p. 85.

53. Washington, J. M. (ed.), 1986, p. 243.

54. King, Coretta Scott, 1983, p. 50.

55. King Jr., Martin Luther, 1989, p. 55.

56. King Jr., Martin Luther, 1988, pp. 55–56.

57. Quoted in Baldwin, L. V., 1992, p. 57.

58. King Jr., Martin Luther, 1964, p. 86.

59. Washington, J. M. (ed.), 1986, p. 206.

60. King Jr., Martin Luther, 1989, p. 50.

61. King, Coretta Scott, 1983, p. 10.

62. Quoted in Baldwin, L. V., 1991, p. 323.

63. King Jr., Martin Luther, 1981, p. 84.

64. King Jr., Martin Luther, 1989, p. 41.

65. Washington, J. M. (ed.), 1986, p. 658.

66. Quoted in Fairclough, A., 1995, p. 13.

67. King Jr., Martin Luther, 1964, p. 31.

68. King, Coretta Scott, 1983, p. 7.

69. Quoted in Frady, M., 2002, p. 63.

70. King Jr., Martin Luther, 1968, p. 40.

71. Quoted in Baldwin, L. V., 1991, p. 322.

72. King Jr., Martin Luther, 1981, p. 51.

73. King Jr., Martin Luther, 1964, p. 92.

74. King Jr., Martin Luther, 1968, p. 200.

75. King Jr., Martin Luther, 1988, p. 41.

76. Quoted in Baldwin, L. V., 1992, p. 7.

77. King Jr., Martin Luther, 1981, p. 25.

78. Quoted in Frady, M., 2002, pp. 45–46.

79. King Jr., Martin Luther, 1981, p. 122.

80. Quoted in Fairclough, A., 1995, pp. 87–88.

81. King Jr., Martin Luther, 1968, p. 50.

82. King Jr., Martin Luther, 1964, p. 133.

83. King Jr., Martin Luther, 1981, p. 104.

84. King, Coretta Scott, 1983, p. 25.

85. King Jr., Martin Luther, 1981, p. 9.

86. Quoted in Frady, M., 2002, p. 39.

87. Washington, J. M. (ed.), 1986, p. 102.

88. King Jr., Martin Luther, 1988, p. 30.

89. King Jr., Martin Luther, 1958, p. 84.

90. King Jr., Martin Luther, 1981, p. 107.

91. Washington, J. M. (ed.), 1986, p. 572.

92. Quoted in Baldwin, L. V., 1992, p. 61.

93. King Jr., Martin Luther, 1989, p. 74.

94. Quoted in Phillips, D. T., 1998, p. 197.

95. King Jr., Martin Luther, 1981, p. 74.

96. King Jr., Martin Luther, 1988, p. 42.

97. King Jr., Martin Luther, 1981, p. 13.

98. Quoted in Baldwin, L. V., 1992, pp. 166–167.

99. Washington, J. M. (ed.), 1986, p. 37.

100. King Jr., Martin Luther, 1981, p. 37.

101. King Jr., Martin Luther, 1988, p. 54–55.

102. Quoted in Phillips, D. T., 1998, p. 1.

103. Washington, J. M. (ed.), 1986, p. 376.

104. King Jr., Martin Luther, 1981, p. 10.

105. King Jr., Martin Luther, 1958, p. 156.

106. King Jr., Martin Luther, 1968, p. 211.

107. King Jr., Martin Luther, 1988, p. 54.

108. Quoted in Baldwin, L. V., 1991, p. 319.

109. King, Coretta Scott, 1983, p. 3.

110. King Jr., Martin Luther, 1964, p. 87.

111. King Jr., Martin Luther, 1981, p. 77.

112. Washington, J. M. (ed.), 1986, p. 234.

113. Quoted in Baldwin, L. V., 1992, p. 251.

114. King Jr., Martin Luther, 1958, p. 164.

115. King Jr., Martin Luther, 1988, p. 59.

116. Washington, J. M. (ed.), 1986, p. 11.

117. Quoted in Baldwin, L. V., 1992, p. 188.

118. Washington, J. M. (ed.), 1986, p. 314.

119. King Jr., Martin Luther, 1981, p. 95.

120. King Jr., Martin Luther, 1989, p. 77.

Bibliography

I. PRIMARY

King, Coretta Scott (1983). *The Words of Martin Luther King Jr. (A Selection).* New York: Newmarket Press.

King Jr., Martin Luther (1958). *Stride Toward Freedom: The Montgomery Story.* New York: Ballantine.

King Jr., Martin Luther (1964). *Why We Can't Wait.* New York: Signet.

King Jr., Martin Luther (1968). *Where Do We Go From Here: Chaos or Community?* New York: Bantam.

King Jr., Martin Luther (1981). *Strength to Love.* Philadelphia: Fortress.

King Jr., Martin Luther (1988). *The Measure of a Man,* Philadelphia: Fortress.

King Jr., Martin Luther (1989). *The Trumpet of Conscience.* New York: Harper *&* Row.

Washington, J. M., ed. (1986). *A Testament of Hope: The Essential Writings and Speeches of Martin Luther King Jr.* New York: HarperSanFrancisco.

II. SECONDARY

Baldwin, L. V. (1991). *There is a Balm in Gilead: The Cultural Roots of Martin Luther King Jr.* Minneapolis: Fortress.

Baldwin, L. V. (1992). *To Make the Wounded Whole: The Cultural Legacy of Martin Luther King Jr.* Minneapolis: Fortress.

Bennett, L. (1968). *What Manner of Man: A Memorial Biography of Martin Luther King Jr.* New York: Johnson Publishing Company.

Fairclough, A. (1995). *Martin Luther King Jr.* Athens, GA: The University of Georgia Press.

Frady, M. (2002). *Martin Luther King Jr.* New York: Viking.

Harding, V. (1996). *Martin Luther King: The Inconvenient Hero.* Maryknoll, NY: Orbis.

Oates, S. B. (1982). *Let the Trumpet Sound: The Life of Martin Luther King Jr.* New York: Mentor.

Phillips, D. T. (1998). *Martin Luther King Jr. on Leadership.* New York: Warner Books.

About the Author

CHARLES RINGMA is regarded by many as a thinker, activist and contemplative. He has written in the areas of the social sciences and philosophy. He has worked as a missioner, researcher, and urban ministry practicioner, and has written numerous books on Christian spirituality. He has lived and worked in Europe, Australia, Asia and Canada, teaching theology and mission at Asian Theological Seminary, Manila and mission studies, philosophy and spirituality at Regent College, Vancouver. As a retired professor he continues to write and teach in various parts of the world.